What It Takes

How Women of Color

Can Thrive Within the

Practice of Law

What It Takes

How Women of Color

Can Thrive Within the

Practice of Law

Monica R. Parker

AMERICAN BAR ASSOCIATION
Defending Liberty
Pursuing Justice

Cover design by ABA Publishing.

The materials contained herein represent the opinions and views of the authors and/or the editors, and should not be construed to be the views or opinions of the law firms or companies with whom such persons are in partnership with, associated with, or employed by, nor of the American Bar Association, unless adopted pursuant to the bylaws of the Association.

Nothing contained in this book is to be considered as the rendering of legal advice, either generally or in connection with any specific issue or case; nor do these materials purport to explain or interpret any specific bond or policy, or any provisions thereof, issued by any particular franchise company, or to render franchise or other professional advice. Readers are responsible for obtaining advice from their own lawyers or other professionals. This book and any forms and agreements herein are intended for educational and informational purposes only.

Printed in the United States of America.

15 14 13   5 4 3

Library of Congress Cataloging-in-Publication Data

Parker, Monica (Monica R.)
    What it takes : how women of color can thrive within the practice of law / Monica R. Parker.
        p. cm.
    Includes index.
    ISBN 978-1-59031-992-5
    1. African American women lawyers. 2. African Americans—Legal status, laws, etc. I. Title.
    KF299.A35P37 2010
    340.082—dc22

2010016766

Discounts are available for books ordered in bulk. Special consideration is given to state bars, CLE programs, and other bar-related organizations. Inquire at Book Publishing, ABA Publishing, American Bar Association, 321 North Clark Street, Chicago, Illinois 60654-7598.

www.ShopABA.org

TABLE OF CONTENTS

ACKNOWLEDGMENTS

First and foremost, thank you to the Father, Son, and Holy Spirit—John 3:16.

Next in line, my loved ones. You're always there for guidance, encouragement, laughter, and love. And most importantly, when I need a kick in the pants. When I hesitated for just a split second at the thought of writing another book, my mom said, "Are you kidding?!" Thanks, Mom!

Thank you to all of the lawyers who shared their stories, both those requesting anonymity and those willing to be identified. Sharing your stories took kindness and courage. (And time away from billable hours!)

Gratitude always for my agent, Jacqueline Hackett, Esq. who brought me to this writing life. I appreciate your continuous dedication to my pursuit of the written word and your ever-ready encouragement.

Much appreciation for my editor, Timothy Brandhorst, for your sharp eye and enthusiastic support. I am grateful.

Monica R. Parker, J.D.
September 1, 2009
Atlanta, GA

INTRODUCTION

You're a woman of color who wants to succeed in the practice of law. If that's what you want, then I believe that you can achieve it.

How can I say that without having met you?

You've already got a history of achievement. Look at what you've accomplished so far on your checklist.

Checklist

- ☑ Take the LSAT
- ☑ Apply to law school
- ☑ Interview for summer clerkship(s)
- ☑ Do excellent work during your clerkship(s)
- ☑ Graduate from law school
- ☑ Pass the bar exam (OK you may not have accomplished this one just yet. But I know you will work very hard to achieve this goal too.)
- ☑ And now you've got the coveted Big Firm offer in hand.

Congratulations! You should be very proud.

I don't use those words lightly. **You should be very proud.** Stop here just a minute and take them in. Soak it up. These are tremendous accomplishments.

I know you overachievers. You're never satisfied. You're always looking off in the distance at whatever spectacular new goals you've set for yourself. That's no way to live.

There will always be new goals, as there should be. But it's also really important to take stock of what you've done so far; otherwise life passes you by. I remember when I graduated from law school. It has been over a decade, but I remember feeling that day as if my heart would burst, I was so proud of myself. You deserve to feel the same.

Feeling it? OK, good, let's move on.

Now you're ready to take on your latest goal. It's the biggest one of your career and life yet: making partner at the Big Firm. It's an exciting and scary challenge. Can you do it?

You look around you at the firm and maybe you don't see that many faces of color. At least not that many at the top. You wonder what that means for you.

It's a good question.

Where Do We Stand?

Part One of this book is an intriguing combination of the past and the present.

In Chapter One, we look at the history of women of color in the law. These pioneers did not have it easy but they managed to accomplish some amazing things.

In Chapter Two, we look at the state of affairs for women of color practicing law today. The findings are startling. As Chapter One demonstrates, we have made a lot of progress in the U.S.A. when it comes to race relations, and yet . . . as Chapter Two illustrates, we still have a long way to go.

Nowhere is this predicament more evident than in the practice of law, especially the practice of Big Firm law. That's the focus of this book. It's about what it takes to achieve greatness as a woman of color in the practice of law at a large firm.

Sure, this book will still be incredibly helpful if you choose to practice in other arenas, whether it's a mid-sized firm or boutique, government, in-house, public interest and so on.

But the focus is Big Firm life. It's the "Holy Grail" of the practice of law for women of color.

Note: If you decide to leave Big Firm life or even the law altogether for the proverbial greener pastures, there's a big, fat chapter for that too. Not all of us are going to stay. Not all of us should stay. Your destiny may be elsewhere.

Who Cares about History? I Need to Know What Works Today!

So why do we have to get into this "moldy old-y" ancient history anyway? Because it's not so long ago actually. And some of it is taking place right now. But most importantly, and as you've no doubt heard many times before, you have to know where you've been to know where you're going. In order to move forward with confidence and capability and to hit your target, you need to know your history.

But don't despair. I promise that the focus of this book isn't how hard it is for women of color in the law. How *not* encouraging would that be? This book focuses on strategy. I talked to several women of color attorneys who have scaled the heights at their firms, so that we could uncover the strategies that will help you achieve your goals at the firm.

Who Is This Book for?

New and Junior Associates. This book has been written especially for young women of color associates. If you're just starting your career at the firm or you've only been there for a year or two, this book is for you.

Mid-Level and Senior Associates. Maybe you've actually been practicing for a while but it sure would be nice to know that others have experienced the joys and agonies you've felt (and perhaps continue to feel). Pull up a chair and put your feet up; you'll enjoy this book. Or maybe you've gotten a bit off track and you're not doing as well as you'd hoped. You can use the book as a compass to get back on track.

Pre-Law and Law Students. If you're a hard-working woman of color who is a pre-law student, law school student, or perhaps you're contemplating a second career in the law, this book is for you too. As you'll see from the stories that partners share, the earlier you can begin to create a positive impression about yourself, the better off you'll be.

Law Firms. This book is also for you if you're curious about what it's like to be a woman of color at a firm, and you're looking for strategies as to how to attract, retain, mentor, and cultivate women of color. It's a terrific resource for understanding how *some* women of color experience practicing law. I emphasize "some" because it would be easy to read what's here and generalize about women of color as a whole. I'd be cautious about doing that since every person has her own unique perspective. I would view the book as a terrific starting point from which to inquire as you talk to individual women of color attorneys.

How to Read this Book

There are a couple of different ways to approach it. I tend to read books from front to back as quickly as possible, and then I read them again to take notes. You can do that. *Or* you can treat it like the handbook it's meant to be. Flip through the Table of Contents and find the chapter that corresponds to what you want to know right now. (My recommendation is <u>not</u> to skip over Part One, however. Or at least make sure to read it at some point. Remember what I said about knowing your history.)

That's why I say start where you like. Pick and choose. The book will be here when you need help. When you're done reading it, put it up on your shelf at work and pull it down when you need it. Highlight passages that interest you, use those yellow arrow tabs firms are so fond of to mark a few sections, write some notes in the margins. It's *your* book.

Most importantly, think of this book as words of wisdom from your big sister. Imagine what it would be like if you had a big sister who was a partner at a Big Firm. Well, now you do!

The women I interviewed for this book care deeply for you. They want very badly for you to succeed. And they're not the only ones.

Guess Who Else Wants You to Succeed?

Yes, yes, I know your mama is delighted and tells everybody about how you're going to be a big-shot attorney. But no, I'm not talking about your mother.

Believe it or not, the firm hired you because they want you to succeed. They're excited about your capabilities and the talents and personality you bring to the firm. Yep, you heard me right but I'll say it again just in case you didn't get it the first time: **Your firm wants you to succeed.**

They may not show it in exactly the right ways but heck, the decision to hire and train you costs them money. You're an investment. They want to make good on that investment.

And as you'll see in the chapter on relationships at work, surprisingly, mentors are everywhere. Sure, look for your own kind, but also don't miss out an incredible opportunity to be trained by someone who's not at all like you.

Most Importantly

The strategies in the book only work though if you use them. Implement. (And, yes, that means if you were hoping that you could just read this book, absorb its wisdom, and be magically teleported to partnership, that's not going to work.)

Who's Writing this Book?

We may have taken different routes, but we both got to the same place: the Big Firm. I'm a product of a prep school education, Advanced Placement classes, a bucket load of extracurricular activities, and parents who insisted that I both believe in and live up to my capabilities. I'm a graduate of Harvard College *cum laude* and Harvard Law School. I've served as a Lecturer of Law at Harvard Law, working with bright, ambitious young minds like yours. I'm a woman of color, African-American to be exact. I worked at two prestigious law firms in Atlanta, GA, both a large firm and a boutique for five years. I know what it's like to succeed within the law . . . and then to make the choice that my fame and fortune lay elsewhere. So now I'm a former practicing attorney.

I'm a coach who works with lawyers. I help unhappy lawyers figure out what's making them unhappy so that they can create engaging, fulfilling, rewarding careers and lives—in or outside of the law.

Oh, Yes, There's Hope!

Sure, as I warned you earlier, this book is going to give you some facts up front that are sobering. But if I left you with just that, you might be discouraged and disheartened. That's not the point.

The point is to show you paths for achieving greatness within the practice of law, in spite of the obstacles. To give you much-needed encouragement and guidance. Hope.

That's what coaching is about. Helping you find your way so that you can create the life and work that you want to have. And hope that it's possible is the very first step.

So take heart. And a deep breath. You've embarked on an incredible journey not for the faint of heart. Your journey will be filled with joy and challenges, wonder and frustrations, exhilaration and trials (no pun intended). How exciting!

A NOTE FOR OVERACHIEVERS

(Which Is Probably Everyone Reading This Book)

I know you. I'm one of you. I read a book like this and I think, "I can do it. I can do it all. I'll get started right now." And then I get overwhelmed and have trouble doing anything.

I can imagine it might be the same for you. There's a lot here. How in the world could you possibly absorb and implement all of it at once?

You can't. So don't try. Pick and choose what feels most relevant for you to learn and practice at this time. (Trust your gut on this one. Or ask someone you trust.) Then do just that—learn and practice those 2 or 3 strategies. As you master them, move on the next.

As someone who must have been very wise once said, "It's a marathon, not a sprint."

PART ONE:

How Did We Get Here?

CHAPTER 1

Our Glorious History

"Well-behaved women seldom make history."

—Laurel Thatcher Ulrich

Imagine what it was like to be one of the *first*. One of the first women of color practicing law in the United States. We think it's hard for us as women of color to practice law today. What was it like back then??

Rather than bombard you with historical information (after all, this isn't a history book), I decided to create a brief timeline. I've included noteworthy dates and a bit of biographical information about the women. As you'll see, clearly, I've chosen the highlights that appeal to me. You want more? Do your own research; it's a fascinating topic.

Note: I couldn't possibly cover the entire history of women of color in the law from "the beginning" until now. That's a book (or series of books) in and of itself. So what we're going to do instead is just take a look at the "firsts," some of the first women of color to practice law in the United States. I say "some" because unfortunately, the history of women of color in the law hasn't always been documented as carefully as we would have liked. Please forgive any omissions; they were unintended.

A super-abbreviated and highly colorful timeline of women of color in the law

1872: Charlotte E. Ray was the first African-American woman admitted to the bar in the United States. In 1869 when Ray was teaching at Howard University (where she was also a student at the time), she applied for admission to the Law Department. But she knew that the school wasn't necessarily interested in admitting women students so she applied as "C.E. Ray" and was admitted. Ray graduated from law school, was admitted to the bar in the District of Columbia in 1872, and opened a practice there. But she couldn't get enough clients because she was a woman of color. Shortly thereafter, she gave up her practice, returned to New York where she was born, got married, and became a teacher.[1] Ray was of mixed racial ancestry including, Native American and European. Her father was a leader in the black community, editing the *Colored American* newspaper in New York City and pastoring at Bethesda Congregational Church.[2]

1882: Violette Johnson was the first African-American woman lawyer permitted to present a case before the U.S. Supreme Court.[3]

1897: Lutie Lytle, the first black female lawyer in the South, was the first black woman admitted to the bars in Tennessee and Kansas. In fall 1898, Lytle announced that she would join the faculty at her alma mater, Central Tennessee Law School. (Lytle was one of two students in her graduating class.) She was the first female law professor of a chartered law school in the world.[4]

1909: Lyda Burton Conley, the first Native American woman attorney in the U.S., was also the first Native American woman admitted to argue a case before the Supreme Court. Burton Conley was actually of Native American and European descent. Her mother was a multiracial member of the Wyandot tribe in Kansas, and her father was a Yankee of Scots-Irish descent. She had three sisters, all of whom were encouraged to pursue education. The sisters lived together all of their lives (one died young), and none of them married. Burton Conley is known for her work to prevent the sale and development of the Wyandot National Burying Ground (also known as Huron Cemetery) in Kansas City.[5]

1929: Rosalind Goodrich Bates received her JD from Southwestern University. She was born to Dr. Rosa Goodrich and Dr. Lorenzo Boido in Sonsonati, El Salvador. She was Secretary and President of the International Federation of Women Lawyers. Dr. Bates, as she was known, was editor of the legal publications *"La Abogada"* (the "Lawyer") and "Lawyers Club Docket" and practiced as a trial lawyer for 20 years. She

[1] http://en.wikipedia.org/wiki/Charlotte_E._Ray
[2] http://womenshistory.about.com/od/aframer18631900/p/charlotte_ray.htm
[3] http://www.nps.gov/brvb/historyculture/reconstruction.htm
[4] http://www.kshs.org/real_people/lytle_lutie.htm
[5] http://en.wikipedia.org/wiki/Lyda_Conley

served as a National Judge Advocate for 15 years and a Judge Pro Tem in the Los Angeles Superior Court.[6]

1930: Martha Lee Ramirez was a graduate of Cheyenne High School and the University of Wyoming. She was the first woman ever to appear and argue a case before the Laramie County District Court; as well as the first woman to appear on the "Roll of Attorneys," the "list of barristers that dates back to 1868, who have taken the oath, permitting them to practice before the Laramie county court."[7]

1933: Josephine Camille Navarro (Woods) was admitted to the Texas State Bar after graduating from Houston Law School. Her practice was focused in the oil & gas industry, having worked for the Land and Title Departments of Standard Oil Co. of Kansas, British American Oil Producing Co., and Shell Oil Company. Woods was active in the Women's Section of the Houston Bar Association.[8]

1937: Elizabeth Ohi was admitted to the bar, becoming the first Japanese-American woman lawyer. She came from a notable pre–war Chicago Japanese-American family. Her father, who arrived in America in 1906 and took a job as a chemist in a steel mill, was a master draftsman and designer of streamlined trains for the Pullman Car Company for several years. His wife was a white woman from Kansas. Kamatsu Elizabeth Ohi was their eldest daughter. She graduated from John Marshall Law School, where she was named class valedictorian. Ohi, dubbed by newspapers a "Nipponese Portia," took a job as a secretary for a local attorney, Max Liss, and later served as legal assistant for future Supreme Court Justice Arthur Goldberg. According to Goldberg, Elizabeth Ohi was arrested by the FBI on the evening of the Pearl Harbor attack. Goldberg's threat to bring an immediate habeas corpus petition on her behalf led to her release. Ohi later served as a Labor Department attorney.[9]

1938: Chiyoko Sakamoto (Takahashi), a Los Angeles native, graduated from American University, Washington College of Law but she was unable to find a job with a law firm. She worked as a legal assistant to a Japanese-American community leader who provided translation serv-

---

[6] The Hispanic National Bar Association's Commission on Latinas in the Profession, *"Las Primeras"* Project

[7] The Hispanic National Bar Association's Commission on Latinas in the Profession, *"Las Primeras"* Project

[8] The Hispanic National Bar Association's Commission on Latinas in the Profession, *"Las Primeras"* Project

[9] "Setting Precedent: Overviewing the History of Nikkei Women in Law," Greg Robinson, Nichei Bei Times, April 17, 2008, http://www.nichibeitimes.com/?p=635.

ices. After being imprisoned in internment camps during World War II, she returned to Los Angeles and was hired by African-American attorney Hugh E. MacBeth as his associate. She later opened her own law office in Los Angeles, Little Tokyo. Sakamoto was also one of the founders of the Japanese-American Bar Association and the California Women's Bar.[10]

1943: Sau Ung Loo Chan, a graduate of Yale Law School, became the first woman of color practicing in Hawaii. Chan was the last of six children for a prominent family that emigrated from China to Hawaii. After graduating from Yale, Chan moved to Hong Kong, got married, and had a child. While in Hong Kong, she worked as an assistant legal counsel for William Hunt & Co.[11] In 1943 she returned to Honolulu and passed the bar. Chan then opened an office in Hawaii. She also contracted with the First Circuit Court of Honolulu to act as a small estate and guardianship attorney on a part-time basis, but that ended up becoming a full-time job. Chan later added an immigration practice to her work.[12]

1973: Dolores Sibonga was the first Filipina-American admitted to the bar of Washington state. She worked as a public defense attorney, a King County Council legislative analyst and then moved to the office of civil rights. Sibonga later became Deputy Director of the Washington State Human Rights Commission. She became the first minority woman to serve on the Seattle City Council in 1980 and served for twelve years total. She unsuccessfully ran for Mayor in 1989. After her Council term expired, she returned to the practice of law.[13]

1984: Wendy Duong graduated from the University of Houston Law Center and received an LLM from Harvard. She was the first Vietnamese-American to clerk with the federal court (1984, Southern District of Texas); the first Vietnamese woman on the bench (municipal court, Houston); and among the few Vietnamese-American law professors in the first and second-tiered law schools. She is currently an Assistant Professor at Sturn College of Law, University of Denver.

---

[10] "Setting Precedent: Overviewing the History of Nikkei Women in Law," Greg Robinson, Nichei Bei Times, April 17, 2008, http://www.nichibeitimes.com/?p=635.

[11] http://the.honoluluadvertiser.com/article/2002/Mar/10/ln/ln26a.html

[12] Called from Within: Early Women Lawyers of Hawaii, Mari J. Matsuda (University of Hawaii Press, 1992), pp. 172–189

[13] http://www.asianjournal.com/voice-of-fil-america/72-voice-of-fil-america/1018-dolores-sibonga-first-filipina-american-lawyer-in-washington-state-first-asian-city-council-member-in-seattle.html

CHAPTER 2

Our Not-So-Glorious Present: The Intersection of Race and Gender

"Not only is another world possible, she is on her way. On a quiet day, I can hear her breathing."

—Arundhati Roy

This chapter is based on the work of the American Bar Association Commission on Women in the Profession (the "Commission"), specifically a study entitled, *Visible Invisibility: Women of Color in Law Firms* (2006).

I first heard of *Visible Invisibility* while attending the Leadership Academy for Women of Color Attorneys (now the Leadership Institute for Women of Color in Law and Business) in Atlanta, GA in 2006. (This conference draws women of color attorneys in law and business from all across the country. For more details, go to www.leadingwomenof color.org.)

Arin Reeves, J.D., Ph.D., Co-Chair of the Commission's study, was presenting some of the findings at the conference. The results were startling and dismal. I already knew that the number of women of color attorneys thinned out appreciably as you went up the ranks. I also know that racism still runs rampant in the United States, including law firms (it's just that it has largely gone undercover). What I didn't know is what a deeply negative impact race and gender issues have had, and continue to have on the advancement of women of color attorneys in their careers. As Reeves and Paulette Brown, Esq., Co-Chair of the Commission's study, said in the Introduction to the report:

"Before undertaking this study, we knew generally what we were going to find, but the depth to which women of color are experiencing and being negatively impacted by their experiences in law firms was not only surprising, it was a jarring wake-up call even to those of us who deal with this issue in our own lives. We are not just losing talent; we are treating talented people in ways that do not speak well of our profession or the values that undergird it."[1]

I'm just going to hit the highlights of the study in this chapter. If you want to see the full report, you can purchase a copy at www.abanet .org/women/woc/wocinitiative.html. Or check with your law firm and if they don't already have a copy, let them cover the cost; you're not the only one at your firm who needs to read it. Also, be sure to download a copy of the follow-up report prepared for the Commission by Reeves, *From Visible Invisibility to Visible Success: Success Strategies for Law Firms and Women of Color in Law Firms* at the same site. This free report contains an excellent set of success strategies obtained from women of color partners.

Impetus for the study

Here's what Pamela Roberts, Chair of the Commission, had to say in "A Note from the Chair:"

"Women of color experience a double whammy of gender and race, unlike white women or even men of color who share at least one of these characteristics (gender or race) with those in the upper strata of management. Women of color may face exclusion from informal networks, inadequate institutional support, and challenges to their authority and credibility. They often feel isolated and alienated, sometimes even from other women.

Previous research focused specifically on either women or on people of color in the legal profession. Recognizing the need for a comprehensive analysis of the unique concerns and experiences of Hispanic, African-

---

[1] Visible Invisibility: Women of Color in Law Firms (ABA Commission on Women in the Profession), p. xi

American, Native American, and Asian-American women in the legal profession, in 2004 the Commission on Women in the Profession undertook a two-part research study composed of a national survey and focus groups."[2]

The stark truth

- The combination of race and gender has had a devastating effect on the lives of women of color, both professionally and personally.
- Women of color don't do as well as white women or even men of color.
- Women of color "are the farthest removed from the successes of white men, who still tend to have the greatest levels of success regardless of where they went to school or their grades in law school."

Things that particularly caught my eye in the study

- The Native American woman attorney who dealt with comments such as, "Where's your tomahawk? Are you going to scalp me?" or "Can I call you Pocahontas?"
- The Asian American woman attorney who is told that she speaks English so well.
- The Latina attorney who realized that only minorities from her firm were assigned to the huge document review she was working on, a project classified by everyone involved as "a dead-end project that was going to last a long time."
- The African-American woman attorney who left her large law firm because she felt "incredibly lonely and isolated. I always felt as though I did not belong."

Phwew. That was rough reading, I know. It was rough for me to read the research and write it.

We're done with this part of the book. It's time to focus on some of the good stuff. You're about to encounter women of color who have not only survived but also thrived at large law firms, in spite of the obstacles. We're going to take a look at the strategies that have helped them succeed, so that *you* can become one of those happy statistics.

---

[2] Visible Invisibility: Women of Color in Law Firms (ABA Commission on Women in the Profession), p. vii.

PART TWO:

The Potential Minefields and Time-Tested Strategies for Getting Around Them

Note

I decided that the best way to get you the information you needed was to go straight to the source: women of color partners. Who better to advise you than those who have made it to the "Promised Land" of partnership?

Their words of wisdom serve as the backbone for this book. So be clear. This isn't theory. These are real-life, time-tested, results-driven strategies.

If I were you, I'd think of my career as a game. Not in the sense that "it's just a game." But in the sense that you're playing the most important game of your life. So what you need when you play the game of life is the best game plan.

Getting to the top of the heap at the Big Firm isn't going to happen just by wishing and hoping. It happens when you think strategically.

And that's what these women have to offer.

Some of the strategies I'm about to share with you in this book may seem obvious to you. That's OK. The issue is not whether you already know about a particular strategy. The issue is whether or not you are *implementing* the strategy.

Take a self-assessment. (Or ask someone you trust.) Be honest with yourself. Are you implementing these strategies? If not, don't beat yourself up. That's a waste of time. Instead, just get started!

CHAPTER 3

It's All About the Work

"Remember, Ginger Rogers did everything Fred Astaire did, but she did it backwards and in high heels."

—Faith Whittlesey

Make no mistake. We're going to get into who you should network with, the importance of building relationships, joining committees, and things like that. BUT it is, has been, and always will be about the work.

Do good work

Every single lawyer I talked to preached about the importance of doing good work and doing it in a timely fashion. If you do good work, partners will remember you the next time a juicy project rolls around and will lobby for you. When you start your career, it may feel like you have so little control. Take advantage of the things over which you *do* have control.

"I didn't miss a deadline. This has changed. When I was coming along, we just didn't. Your hours. Never miss your hours. That's objective. Deadlines—those are objective. So much is subjective. Focus on anything you can control. If the deadline is Friday, turn it in on Wednesday."

—Allegra Lawrence-Hardy, Partner,
Litigation, Sutherland, Asbill & Brennan, Atlanta, GA

If you do good work, when you make mistakes, because you *will* make mistakes, that good work gives you a cushion, a margin for error. A partner is more likely to say, "Well, Sally, has always done a good job for me before. Everybody makes mistakes." Versus "Every time I give Sally a project there are always errors." That's when you become "Sally who?" the next time there's a good project.

Don't let your ego get in the way of your success

"I remember a time I was stuck in a basement in Scotland doing due diligence. I didn't even get to see Scotland, well, not that much of it. I was stuck in a basement with terrible files. All I wanted to do was be out on the street having fun.

A friend [told me], 'As low as it may seem, when you go through those boxes, you're the only person who knows what's in them. You're the expert on what's in those boxes.' If that doesn't matter to you, then you won't be at a firm for very long. That's fine. I wasn't either. But I took that seriously. The acquisition of knowledge is powerful. That will help you.

Upon reflection on the Scotland due diligence, I realized that I hadn't let my ego get in the way."

—Rhonda Adams Medina, Senior Vice President, Business and Legal Affairs, Deputy General Counsel, Nickelodeon/ MTV Networks Kids and Family Group, New York, NY

So we get it. Do good work. No task is too small.

The primary question on your mind is *how* do you get good work? Yes, yes, we know how to get the crappy projects. (Just wait for someone to stop by your office with them.) But how do you get the good stuff?

It all starts before you're even a summer associate

*"**The process of building your reputation starts when you interview for your position as a summer associate.** When you interview for your position, if you're knocking the socks off the person who's interviewing you, they're going to go back, they're going to say, 'Hey I met this great candidate at this school. We've got to have her.' Then that builds to you getting your callback. You impress those people, same thing happens. 'This is a great candidate. We've got to get her here.' And so when you accept your offer to come to that firm, they're excited about you coming, even as a summer person.*

And then as a summer person, you're getting to get the work that you like and the practice group that you like because the firm wants to recruit you. You're someone they want to join the firm, so they're going to work

*with you to try to get you good assignments. **When you get good assignments in your summer position and you do an excellent job on those, that creates your reputation even before you join.** So that when you join as a first year, you are already being seen as a potential star lawyer.*

*It's almost like it feeds on itself. Because you're coming in with a good reputation from the work you did as a summer associate, you are getting an opportunity to maybe have meatier assignments earlier than . . . someone who's coming in who hasn't really made an impact or impression one way or the other. **And so I think it's important to view your career as starting well before you even show up on the first day of your first year.***"

—Angela Payne James, Partner,
Intellectual Property Litigation, Alston & Bird

*Emphasis added to make sure you caught the especially juicy bits.

Now let's look at some specific strategies.

Strategy #1: Camp out in the lane

I promise I won't be using sports analogies throughout the book. It's just that this one seemed apropos. And for those of you who have no idea what "camping out in the lane means," here's a definition from Dummies.com (no insult intended, it was just the first helpful entry in Google that popped up):

*"Three seconds: No part of an offensive player may remain in the free throw lane for more than three consecutive seconds unless the ball is being shot. If the shot hits the rim, the player standing in the lane gets a new three seconds. Thus if you happen to be **camping out in the lane** [bold added] for two seconds and the shot hits the rim, you may remain in the lane for another three seconds.*

After a player steps out of the lane, the count resets, and [s]he can re-enter the lane for another three seconds. A player can go in and out of the lane as often as [s]he likes."

More information than you ever wanted about basketball terminology, yes, I know.

But as I'm using the term in this book, "camp out in the lane" means stop by the partner's office regularly and ask how you can help.

Yes, I know I said earlier that your practice group is excited that you're there. But the partners in your group have a lot on their minds. Rather than waiting for them to come find you, go out and find them:

"[The partner who ended up being my mentor, particularly in the early years, tells a story about how I made him adopt me. [laughs] Lane Dennard (retired partner from King & Spalding) was the only partner in our group at that time who practiced traditional labor law, the union side of it full time. And that was something I was really interested in. And so apparently I came to his office every few days until he had to give me something, to make me go away. [laughs] And I assume he's telling the truth. I don't remember pestering him to death."

—Lovita Tandy, Partner,
Labor & Employment, King & Spalding, Atlanta, GA

Learning points from Strategy #1:

- **Know what you want.** Tandy first identified that she wanted to do traditional labor law. She then identified who was doing traditional labor law. It's so obvious that it's easy to gloss over this one. You first have to know what you want and figure out who's doing it. If you don't know what you want and who's doing it, you're going to end up with projects that don't appeal to you.
- **Go get it.** Then Tandy, well, camped out in the lane. She introduced herself and made herself available to Dennard. OK, so maybe you don't have to check in as often as she did. But there's nothing wrong and everything right with going after what you want. Go by their office (and go by often) to let them know that you're available for projects and how much you want to work with them.

Strategy #2: Go to the Wall for the Partners You've Selected

That's probably another sports analogy isn't it? Well this one isn't my fault. Tandy uses those very words below and again, they seemed on point.

What does it mean to "go to the wall" in this context? It means that you do everything that is humanly possible to do an extraordinary job on the partner's project and to do so in a timely fashion.

"Once I started working with Lane—and there was another partner at the time who was sort of winding down his practice—I went to the wall for them. If they needed something, I did it. I don't care what else anybody else had for me to do. I did it and I did theirs first.

But I knew they had my back on that too. And I was very explicit about it. I would say, 'OK . . . Lane, I understand that you need this by the end of the day. [Another partner] needs this other thing by the end of the day.' And he'd say, 'Don't worry about it. I'll take care of it.' "

—Lovita Tandy

Learning points from Strategy #2:

- **Do whatever it takes.** You know, I talk to so many lawyers who just "get by" at work. That's symptomatic of a larger problem we won't get into here but the point is, don't do that. If you want the opportunity to take on engaging projects, work with the partners you want, and develop your career, then you need to give it everything you've got.
- **Be selective.** Notice that Tandy didn't say that she "went to the wall" for everybody. In fact, she used Dennard and another partner as a shield so that she didn't have to do that. Pick your champions. Work really hard for them. And in return they will protect you. But be sure to do just as Tandy did and negotiate for that kind of protection. Don't make any assumptions; discuss your workload with these partners and have them make the choices about what comes first. You shouldn't be making those kinds of decisions early on in your career.

Strategy #3: Be Anal about Deadlines

"I think for me it's really being an Army brat. [chuckles] When my parents told us to do something, we had to do it and we had to do it in the timelines. I was really always a person who would rather get a B on a paper than get an extension and get an A because my parents didn't play extensions when I was growing up. I mean it was just how I was raised. So I was always very anal about deadlines. As I got older, and was here [at the firm] longer, I would see that there were people who would turn stuff in late. I just never even knew that was an option. I'll tell you the truth, I probably didn't even know it was an option in college until end of sophomore year. It never occurred to me that you could do that."

—Lovita Tandy

Learning points from Strategy #3:

- **Forget about skipping classes and asking for extensions.** We're in the real world now. And how you handle deadlines says every-thing about you. Meet them. If you're given a deadline, meet it (or beat it). If you're asked to offer a deadline, offer one that you can make.
- **A little tip I learned at the firm.** Offer a deadline that gives you a bit of cushion. That way when you finish the project early, you can turn it in and impress the heck out of the partner with your timeliness.

Strategy #4: Have a positive attitude

"As a junior, your key asset is having a good attitude. Of course, there's also working hard and paying attention to detail. When you do these things, people want to work with you, and learn to trust you, and to rely on you. This is how you will get more substantive responsibilities over time."

—Tracy High, Partner, Litigation, Criminal Defense and
Investigations, Sullivan & Cromwell, New York, NY

Learning Points from Strategy #4:

- **Have a good personality.** This issue will come up again in the chapter on developing relationships at work because it's vital. People like being around people who have a good attitude. Those are the people they want to give assignments to; work closely with. After all, if you have to spend a lot of time with someone, wouldn't you want to spend it with someone who is pleasant, eager to do the work, and pays close attention to their work?
- **It's all about liking you and trusting you.** As High says, your ability to get good work is based upon your ability to do the work that you *do* get well and with a positive attitude. Do well on the small things, maintain that positive attitude, and you get larger projects.

Strategy #5: Learn as much as you can

"I'm trying to think if I ever said, 'No.' [to a project]. I don't think I ever did. My perspective was to do everything with as much enthusiasm as you can. Try to learn as much as you can. I could see how busy the partners were. I tried to learn about the business of law firms . . . I embraced everything. It didn't matter."

—Lisa Kobialka, Partner, Intellectual Property,
King & Spalding, Silicon Valley, CA

Learning Points from Strategy #5:

- **Be a sponge.** There's so much to learn. Although we were taught in law school to pretend as if we know the answer to everything (and firms often encourage this as well), take on the mindset of a perpetual student. Tackle everything you're given as if you want to learn it inside out. Be like Kobialka and learn about the business of law firms. Embrace everything.

Is It *Ever* Appropriate to Say "No?"

"I think the first time I might have said 'no' to an assignment was probably somewhere between third and fourth year. I was splitting practice groups for a little bit when I started. I was in IP Litigation and Trial Practice. And that became a problem because you have nobody who is over your workload.

So if you've got a summary judgment brief due from a partner in Trial Practice and a summary judgment brief due from a partner in IP Litigation and they're both due at the same time, you just have to get them both done. And I was running into that a lot. And I think at some point just from timing and knowing I wasn't going to be able to get something done and do a good job, I simply said, 'I'm really sorry. I can't do this because of all of these various things I have on my plate.'

But I didn't say 'no' very often. Because, of course, you want to succeed and you know that people want to view you as being reliable and a go-to person. Saying 'no' a lot isn't going to create that impression. So generally speaking, if I felt I could do it, I would do it. As you get more senior too you have a better sense of what can you really do—after you've tried to please everyone and do ten assignments at once a few times and you realize that's really not going to work out.

At some point you realize you are better off saying up front, 'Here's the situation. Unless there's some flexibility there, I'd be concerned that I wouldn't be able to do a great job for you.'

And also if you're doing that when you're more senior, you've already built the foundation, you've already built your reputation, you've already built relationships with these people. So when you're saying it, they know that you really mean that. And you're not just trying to avoid work or you're doing it because you're lazy or whatever. Whereas if you're doing that as a first year and you haven't built that reputation, people don't know where you're coming from.

I think by the time I started to say these things, I had the credibility to say them."

—Angela Payne James

So does that mean you can *never* say "No?" Let's look at a few scenarios and see how the pros handled them.

Scenario A: You Said "Yes" to Everything and Now You've Got Too Much to Do

You're getting good work and doing good work, lots of it. In fact, so much that you're getting overwhelmed. Heck, you got what you wished

19

for but you're wondering if there's any way to slow this train down. At this rate, you're going to have to put a cot in your office since you're going to be here all night, every night. Seriously.

Dare you politely say "Thanks, but no thanks" to the next assignment you receive? Or do you just smile and suck it up? After all, the last thing you want is a reputation as "The Young Associate Who Dared to Say "No." (Imagine an echo on the "No" here.) What's a savvy girl to do?

Option #1: Explain the Situation

"I did it [said 'No'] in the context of—'I would love to help but here's where I'm at right now. I couldn't do it in a way that it needs to be done.' "

—Elizabeth Reza, Partner,
Corporate, Ropes & Gray LLP, Boston, MA

Option #2: Ask a Partner to Help You Prioritize

"I was exhausted that first year because I didn't think that I could say 'no.' [A couple of people] that helped me were my associate-mentor, Scott Blews and [his wife who was also an associate], Shelly Blews.

I think there's a real art to saying "no." And the lesson that Shelly taught me that I think is just dead-on, is just dead-true: Do not make a decision. Do not choose one partner over another. Do not try to resolve a conflict on your own because it's a [battle] you won't win.

Everybody [else] had that attitude of you've got to take more, you've got to take more, you've got to take more. Except Shelly. And I saw that it didn't negatively impact her. I wasn't here a couple of months when I was at lunch with her and she said, 'I have summary judgment brief due for Lane and one due for Bill and they're both due at the end of the week so I had to go in and ask them "Which one do you want me to do?' "

"What Scott taught me was you don't say 'no.' What you say is essentially, 'Gosh, I have been waiting my entire career to do this boring document review for you. If only I did not have all this other work, I would get it to you today. Since I have all this other work, I can get it to you in a timeframe that I know is completely unacceptable to you but will make you go ask someone else.' "

—Lovita Tandy

Scenario B: You Said "Yes" to Everything and Now You Don't Have Anything Good

You came in as "Eager Beaver" (A.K.A. "Gunner") with your hand raised first for any and all projects and boy, did the partners and senior associates ever take advantage. You've got piles of stuff to do. Document reviews, research projects, non-billable stuff like article research and writing. In other words, you've got a sneaking suspicion that this is definitely not the good stuff. Have you accidentally relegated yourself to this kind of work for the rest of your life or is there a way out of this tunnel of paper?

Option #1: Next Time, Don't Be So Quick to Raise Your Hand

"[They say, 'You're] not supposed to say no.' And I think for most of us, we hear that as being then I have to say 'yes.' White males are far more flexible with those rules. I think the average white male learns sooner that there are things in between.

You get an email, and you know, we used to get those emails when we were first years: 'Alright, I've got the crappiest project in the whole wide world. Who can do this for me?' And not just women of color, every woman hit 'Reply' right away and said, 'Me, me, me, me, me!' Uh uh. White male is going to wait 3 hours until he knows, might even come by your office just to make sure you're doing it and then he's going to volunteer and say, 'Oh, I'm so sorry. If something like that comes up again, please think of me first.' Right?"

—Lovita Tandy

Scenario C: You Keep Getting Stuck Working for an Associate Who Is, How Shall I Put This Delicately, the Other Name for a Donkey

It's your worst nightmare. Somehow you've managed to become the number one whipping boy, er, girl for the biggest jerk associate in your group. You can't stand this guy. He criticizes everything you do. It's demoralizing. And what's worse, every time you turn around he's handing you something else to do. Is there any way out of this?

Option #1: Find work, any work, from anywhere else

Remember those partners you've selected as the ones you want to do work for? March down to their office right now and offer your assistance. On anything.

"There was a senior associate I did not like working for. And so whatever it was he had for me to do, I mean sometimes he would call me and say, 'Lovita, I need for you to do x, y, and z' and I'd go down the hall to a partner who I know he's not going to mess with and say, 'Excuse me, can I

21

wash your car?' I mean I don't care what it is you need me to do, as long as it's not for him. And then I would call him back and say, 'Ooh, mm, yeah, if this person who doesn't like you and can fire you at a moment's will hadn't just given me a big project to do, I would love to help you but I can't.' "

—Lovita Tandy

CHAPTER 4

Relationships at Work

"There is a special place in Hell reserved for women who don't help other women."

—Madeleine Albright

I'm about to say something that might seem really obvious to you but bear with me. (Not everyone knows this.) You've got to have mentors. You've got to have people who can show you the landmines and how to avoid stepping on them. You need people you can go to when you have questions and concerns that you trust will provide you with good answers. You need someone who will let you cry on their shoulder. You need someone who will strategize with you. And I said "mentors" plural because you won't find all of this in one person, nor should you expect to do so.

Let me put it bluntly for emphasis: I doubt you'll succeed without mentors.

I think instinctively we all know this. The first question though is *how* do you get them?

Strategy #1: Start by doing good work.
Yes, we're back to that again.

"For me I think it's about doing excellent, quality work. And I have always got your back. If you're in a ditch, you know I will pull you out. I'm not going to go golfing with you, I'm not going to go drinking with you, but if you need it done and you need it done right, come to me. And you would be surprised, you know, really if given that choice most part-

ners would rather have somebody who will get it done and get it done right."

—Lovita Tandy

Learning Points from Strategy #1:

- **You don't have to be their golfing buddy.** So that's interesting. I would have thought if you're not going to play golf with a partner or go drinking with them, in other words, socialize with them, you're not going to be able to build a quality relationship. That's not the case at all.
- **Be their go-to person at work.** But of course. The basis for this relationship after all is work. If they know that they can rely on you under any circumstances and again, you're going to do good work and go to the wall for them on it, well, heck, you're the natural choice when this partner is looking around for someone to mentor.

Strategy #2: Be likeable

Yes, we're back to that again. But I'll bet you can think of a lot of robots walking around your office who missed Basic Training 101 in people skills. Just think how easy it is then to make yourself stand out in a positive way.

"It probably goes back to [the fact that] people like to be with people of like-mind. Someone they feel a level of comfort with, they can bond with."

—Simone Boayue-Gumbs, Shareholder,
Financial Institutions, Greenberg Traurig, Miami, FL

"I think if you do good work first and foremost, your work will speak for itself. But I think there's a package that goes along with that—being personable, being able to have relationships, building relationships. A lot goes into being a good practitioner, having interpersonal skills."

—Charmaine Slack, Partner, Employee Benefits and
Executive Compensation, Tax, Jones Day, New York, NY

"Be liked. Be a personable person. Someone who smiles even on bad days, someone who people want to be around. Who laughs at stupid jokes.

For women it might mean putting up with crap you don't normally want to put up with. Harmless fun among the guys that a woman would say, 'I never.' You need a thicker skin. People have to feel comfortable being themselves around you."

—Sulee Clay, Partner, Corporate and Securities,
DLA Piper, Washington, D.C.

24

"When I worked in investment banking and it was booming, we had our pick of the top kids. Someone told me, 'Don't just pick the smartest. Pick the person you wouldn't mind being stuck in coach with going to China.' I endeavored to be that person."

—Rhonda Adams Medina

Learning Points from Strategy #2:

- **Be personable.** Makes sense, doesn't it? Strive to be likeable, to be someone that others want to be around. Be polite, kind, thoughtful, warm—you know, all the stuff your mom taught you! Don't you prefer to be around people like that? Partners are no different. They'd much rather work with associates who have a good personality.
- **Don't be an "angry black woman." Or at least, hide it.** One partner (who shall remain nameless) jokingly referred to how being an angry black woman is a part of her nature that she has to keep a lid on at the office. After all, no one likes to feel put on the defensive. The majority race is not going to be too comfortable with you if they feel like you have a chip on your shoulder, if they sense that you blame them personally for slavery, Jim Crow, historical gender-based discrimination, and the catastrophic consequences of all of those events.

Strategy #3: Get your name (and face) out there

"With so much technology it's easy to sit in your office and do your work thinking that you're doing all that you can. It really helps to put in the face time. If you can bring a draft over [to the partner] and just say, 'Hi, here it is and let me know if there's anything I can do.' That takes two minutes and it puts you in the person's path. We all tend to forget it makes a difference to see somebody."

—Carmen Toledo, Partner, Toxic Tort, King & Spalding, Atlanta, GA

"[Get to know] management. The heads know me, have talked to me. They want to see me succeed. That's important.

It's about finding out what they care about and trying to execute. Hitting your numbers. Doing what I was supposed to do as an associate.

Not jumping around firms, that mercenary crap. Chasing dollars. That's not good in times of famine. They don't know you. They feel I've grown up here."

—Sulee Clay

25

"I went out of my way to get work with people I hadn't run into who I thought were important to have exposure with me. I literally went and knocked on their doors.

Be very thoughtful about who to work with. Have some diversity and variety. It's not putting all of your eggs in one basket. It's making sure people know your name."

—Elizabeth Reza

Learning Points from Strategy #3:

- **See and be seen.** Don't hide in your office. As Toledo suggests, hand assignments to the assigning partner in person. Stop by a colleague's office to see if there's something you can assist them on. Make an effort to show them the person that's attached to all of this great work that's getting done—you!
- **Be strategic.** Find out who's influential and go out of your way to work with them. Consider the advice of diversity consultant, Vernā Myers:

"Sometimes people get bent out of shape [about the fact that a partner in their group seems to gravitate toward the young, white male associates]. They may have less to worry about than they think. Who cares if the partner is friends with the associate? That partner may not be influential. Why worry about it?

Who are the influential partners? Figure out who the important people are in [your] department. What can [you] do to create connections?

What is true is that some people find it hard to deny help. If you can become indispensable to the right partner . . . Because, by the way, women and people of color tend to put their heads down and work hard and then one day they look up and find out the partner they've been doing all of their work for is not influential or he's leaving. Working really hard is just the fundamental. It's basic. Everyone is expected to do that. You're not going to necessarily advance by only doing good work. You have to focus on relationship development.

The other thing: don't make assumptions. People are interested and willing to support you; they're just not sure how you feel about them. You say, 'That partner is always talking sports with that associate. Why him and why not me?' Have you stopped by their office and brought up sports, or are you expecting the partner to come your way?

Make no assumptions about who can support you. In fact assume everyone can regardless of who they are. It's true that the partner may go towards the relationships that are easy, where they see affinities. But you don't know what affinities you have unless you explore them."

—Vernā Myers, JD, Principal, Vernā Myers Consulting Group

- **Find out what they care about.** You know the expression, "Food is the way to man's heart?" That should be your job: finding out the way to management's heart. One partner mentioned that one of her senior partners had a pet pro bono project. You can bet she's helping him with this project. And you can bet he thinks highly of her.

Strategy #4: Think outside the box

"[My] relationship with Lane Dennard—his thing was that he was really old school and saw a part of his job as being a mentor, and so, particularly with the Labor work, he would only work with a few people at a time. So either you got in or you didn't.

And in fact there had been other minorities who had been on this team who were no longer on the team who told me to stay away from him. [They told me,] 'Go work with that Jewish man down the hall.' Lane is from South Georgia and he has a strong South Georgia accent and I think, you know, you assume he's this big redneck. But quite frankly I had probably more in common with him than any of the other partners. He came from like a middle class background, started out lower-middle class, parents went to school while he was watching his younger brothers and sisters sort of thing. So I think economically we came from about the same place. He had been in the military, which was similar to my background. And I think people do look for themselves in their protégés but for him he was looking for somebody who had that fire in the belly and was sort of first generation professional like him."

—Lovita Tandy

"My mentors have always been white men frankly. Part of it is there's not as many women out there. Plus the women have so much on them. Time is valuable. They're juggling so much."

—Lisa Kobialka

Toledo agrees:

"My mentors are white men. Because there's no Puerto Rican woman, I'm the only one here. There are a few other women litigators but it's so

27

unfair to them. They can't be expected to be everything to everyone. It's unfair to expect them to be mentors to everyone."

—Carmen Toledo

Learning Points from Strategy #4:

- **Mentors come in all shapes, colors, and sizes.** Yes, I know ideally you'd find a mentor who's just like you. And the folks I interviewed for this book agree that you should definitely seek out such mentors.

  But I guarantee that you will be making a massive mistake if you limit your search to just women of color. Why? Well, as Kobialka and Toledo say above, the obvious reason is that there just aren't that many. The less obvious reason is that your ability to learn isn't limited to learning from someone of your own background. Anyone can be a teacher, trusted advisor, wise counsel, friend.

- **And I do mean all shapes, colors, and sizes.** You know who helped me out the most when I started at my first firm? The legal secretaries and paralegals. In my case, my own secretary wasn't particularly interested in helping me; she preferred to dote on the high-powered white male partner she was assigned to. Fortunately, two African-American legal secretaries took pity on me and took up my secretary's slack.

  Some of these folks have been there for years (read as, they were there when you were playing with building blocks and didn't know what a lawyer was), can do your job with their hands tied behind their back (surprise, surprise, a law school education does not translate into practice experience), and know everything there is to know at the firm. Befriend them and reap the benefits, or at the very least, it would behoove you not to antagonize them.

Toledo agrees:

> *"I made my best friends with a lot of the staff and a lot of the paralegals. They will cover your back."*

—Carmen Toledo

Strategy #5: Go towards the partners everyone else tells you stay away from

Sounds crazy, I know. But I heard it more than once. Remember, that's what senior associates told Tandy about her mentor (see story in Strategy #4 above). Here's another example:

"People actually said to me, 'You don't want to work with this guy.' He's not doing the hot stuff. I said, 'I want to learn it all.'

This guy was a micromanager. It was real stressful. I'd describe it as a haze. A man who's a perfectionist, you can never make him happy. You do ten drafts before the client sees one. He's talking down to you: 'Where's your brain?' You start to question yourself.

Once you're in good stead, they start to trust you, so I gritted it out.

Sometimes I needed a break, so I'd go take a deal where they didn't really manage me.

A lot of micromanagers back off once they trust you. Now we're colleagues and friends. He recently marked up one of my documents: 'Utterly incomprehensible.' [laughs] He's still training me.

Here's the difference between succeeding [in the practice of law] versus not: You want to find someone who's interested in you developing as a lawyer. He couldn't bill all the time he spent [training] me.

If you can find someone who's a rainmaker and who's not racist or sexist, who thinks you're smart, will spend time teaching you and you survive the haze, that's what you need."

—Sulee Clay

Learning Points from Strategy #5:

- **If everyone says do one thing, do the opposite.** As I said, I heard this principle more than once. Yes, the person everyone is running from is obviously difficult. But difficult can sometimes mean that there is a valuable teacher underneath the apparent insensitivity and demanding nature. After all, if they're taking the time to critique your work (even if the criticism seems harsh), that means that they're trying to teach you.

Strategy #6: When an opportunity presents itself, step up to the plate

"When I was a third year, I got a great assignment with the head of the Litigation group. As it began to get more complex, he asked me, 'Do you want to get a senior associate to help you with this or can you handle the responsibility?'

That was him giving me an opportunity. Instead of being scared, I thought, 'Let me step up to the plate. This is my opportunity to function directly with a partner.'

I really appreciate him saying, 'Do you want this opportunity?' I have worked with him throughout the years, and have learned so much from him.

29

After that there was another case with another partner. It ended up being my most time-intensive case. I still work on pieces of it to this day. He also took an interest in me growing and developing. We talked about the things I could do better, the things I needed to learn, the law as a business. He took me to meet the CEO, the Board, to do presentations. I was getting to do things at a junior level.

It was a quid pro quo. My end of the bargain is that I did the best job I could."

—Tracy High

Learning Points from Strategy #6:

- **Carpe diem.** As you can see from the story above, High didn't take on this challenge as a first year; she was a third year. She trusted in her capabilities; you can trust in yours. These kinds of opportunities are like gold in your career. Not only did High prove herself to the partner, but also she developed relationships with other partners who brought her on to their big cases and exposed her to some valuable experiences. Believe in yourself and seize these opportunities when they are presented to you.

Strategy #7: Develop your own "Board of Directors"

"I have always believed in a 'Board of Directors.' You don't need just one friend. It's often too much to ask one person to be your everything. It's great to have a mentor who looks like you. There are issues that are unique to you. But women make a mistake to think that only women of color partners can mentor you."

—Allegra Lawrence-Hardy

Angela Payne James would agree. Notice the progression as Payne James advanced in her career; her Board of Directors grew as she grew:

"When I first came, Cari Dawson was assigned as my Associate Contact. Cari, who is also an African-American female, took that pretty seriously. She's always gone out of her way to play that role for me from my summer on.

And then I have a lot of informal mentoring relationships with the more senior black folks who were here at the time. . . . There was a community of African-American attorneys who were supporting each other in their development in the firm: Chris Ford, Bernard Taylor, Candace Smith, Debra Sydnor.

30

Really now we're all kind of like peers but at the time if you're a year apart or two years apart, that was enough for them to be an informal mentor to me and I viewed it that way.

And then of course I think Frank Smith [head of Payne James' practice group] became a mentor because I asked him to be my mentor. Now that doesn't necessarily mean that he swooped me under his wing and we have heart-to-heart conversations. What it basically meant is that he would help me strategically think about the kinds of cases I should be on and he was in a position to help get me on those cases because he was the practice group leader.

And then Mike Kenny—we worked together on [a big] case and he's been a mentor and someone I can go to since then.

You need a lot of different mentors who serve different roles. I do not go and cry to Frank Smith and Mike Kenny about frustrations. If I need a professional question and I need to have it answered, then I might go to them. Whereas when I was more junior, I might go to Cari Dawson and say, 'This is frustrating. How do I handle this?' Or I might go to Deb Sydnor and have the more heart-to-heart talk."

—Angela Payne James

Kobialka echoes Payne James' advice:

"You need different mentors for different things. Certain mentors mentor you but it's not a direct thing. You sit back and watch them do things. Ask them. That may be a mentor. They have no idea they're mentoring me.

Other mentors are people I can go to and ask questions. They spend time to help me refine my legal skills. They have been great because it allowed me to become a strategic thinker."

—Lisa Kobialka

Here's how High describes it:

"Find more than one mentor. Your mentors will feed different aspects of your personality. They all need to be fed if you're going to thrive. . . . It's essential for your long term professional growth to feel like you have support for every part of your identity."

—Tracy High

Learning Points from Strategy #7:

- **Mentors serve different roles.** As you can see from the stories above, these attorneys have mentors to talk to about cases, mentors

31

to talk to about challenges, and mentors with whom they can have deeply personal conversations. One person cannot, should not, and will not be everything to you. So don't expect that. Instead, figure out what you need and be strategic about finding people who can give it to you.

- **Mentors can be formal and informal.** Firms make it a practice these days to assign mentors to new associates. Those are your formal mentors. It's a good practice and to be commended. It shouldn't surprise you though that those relationships don't always gel. Whether two people connect and how they connect are a bit of a mystery. If you're not getting what you need from your formal mentors, go get some others.

Strategy # 8: Look for mentors both inside and outside of your practice area

"When I decided to step off [the partnership] track, the partner with whom I did my most work was my sounding board. When seven or eight years later I [decided to get back on the partnership track], he was my sounding board. He'd say things like, 'You need to be strategic;' 'Here's what to say;' 'Here's what to put in your pro forma.' "

—Carmen Toledo

"I think it's good for people to be active in the firm as much as you can because you want to get to know people outside your practice group. Because the influential people in the firm are not all going to be in your practice group. In many instances they're not. And so you have to find a way to get to know those people. And doing things like being on the Hiring Committee and being on the Associate Committee, which I did, and coordinating the summer program and going to various events help you at least get to know those other people. And that can translate into getting to work with them. And then if you're working with them you have an opportunity to impress them and do great work and build relationships."

—Angela Payne James

Learning Points from Strategy #8:

- **Get involved in firm activities.** They definitely run the gamut, so you should be able to find a project or committee that appeals to you. As Payne James said, it's a terrific way to develop relationships, not only from the work that you do together on the committee but also the potential work you could do together on cases.

- **Influential people don't just exist inside your practice group.** It's easy to develop tunnel vision. "Why should I get to know people outside of my group when I'm trying to make partner in Trial Practice or Labor & Employment or whatever?" Because it's not just partners in Trial Practice, Labor & Employment or whatever who sit on the Partners Committee. And not everybody in your group is an influential person, partner or no. How much better are your chances for partnership going to be if you have interacted in a positive and significant way with a number of influential people across the board?

Myers, agrees:

> *"Build relationships throughout the firm. That may mean being on a committee or taking advantage of some opportunity or event that goes across the firm."*

> —Vernā Myers, J.D., Principal,
> Vernā Myers Consulting Group

As one Diversity Committee Chair told me when I asked her about the importance of developing relationships both inside and outside of your practice group:

> *"[When one associate makes partner, there are other associates in her group who don't make it who are wondering,] 'Well wait why did I not make it and she make it?' And I think it's because [that candidate] worked for those people [on the Partners Committee], they know [her], they can speak [about her] personally as opposed to just relying on the practice group leader who will come in and present all of the candidates and say, 'This person would be really great.' But [the people on the Partners Committee] don't know them so they may not get that extra little benefit of the doubt that if literally 7 of the 9 people [this associate has] worked with on an actual case or on some committee or volunteered with, then they can speak personally about [her]."*

> —Anonymous Attorney

Strategy #9: Look for mentors outside your firm

"I had really great mentors outside of the firm. One was a friend of a friend. He was a partner in a New Jersey firm. Two were my former law school professors. They [all] helped a lot. They would give me advice about how to maintain my sanity, other ways to approach difficult situa-

33

tions, advice about various avenues I could take when I decided to leave [the practice of law]."

—J. Shontavia Jackson, Professor of Law,
Loyola University College of Law

"I had to reach externally. Karol Mason [a partner at Alston & Bird] is one of my mentors. There was a community of black partners in Atlanta. They read my memos, offered psychological support, talked about the fears we have.

I was so involved with GABWA (the Georgia Association of Black Women Attorneys). I think . . . that was God choosing that for me. Some of my best friends were members. It was an incredible source of support."

—Allegra Lawrence-Hardy

"There were no black partners when I was a young senior associate so I reached outside the firm. I went to a panel on rainmaking. Pauline Schneider [a partner at Orrick Herrington & Sutcliffe LLP] was on the panel. I connected with her later.

We had conversations—'This is how you deal with the credit system.' 'This is how you ask for credit, this is what you say.' Lots of pep talks."

—Sulee Clay

Learning Points from Strategy #9:

- **You can't always get what you want . . . at the firm.** I know you want to be mentored by at least one, if not more, women of color attorneys. If they're not at your firm, go find them elsewhere! Meet the senior associates and partners at other firms. Take them to lunch and ask them questions. Keep in touch. And obviously, they don't just have to be attorneys. J. Shontavia Jackson relied on her law school professors as well.

Strategy #10: You don't even have to know your mentors

"For me a lot of people I didn't even know personally [but] read about, knew about, observed how they were in professional life, I admired them. I wanted to be like them.

I worked at my tribal college nine years before I went to law school. Selma Thomas was the president of the college. She was smart, Native [American], educated, and professional at all times. She dressed well, took care of herself, spoke well. When she came into a room, she had presence. She was a good leader. She brought people together and had a good sense of humor, which is important. I'm not sure I've ever had a conversation with her about that.

It's particularly important in certain kinds of communities—in inner cities, on reservations. There were not a lot of role models. Growing up I knew one lawyer in town who was also a tribal member. I thought, 'Wow, she did it.' Nobody in my family went to college. I had to figure it out along the way. It was necessary to look outside. I bought Wilma Mankiller's [the first female chief of the Cherokee Nation] book. Never met her. LaDonna Harris [nationally recognized advocate on behalf of Native Americans] was another one."

—Danelle Smith, Partner, Native American Law,
Fredericks Peebles & Morgan LLP, Omaha, NE

Learning Points from Strategy #10:

- **You don't have to know them to let them mentor you.** You can learn a lot from observing others, even people you don't know. As Smith mentioned, she considered mentors to be those she knew but didn't have actual mentoring relationships or those she didn't know at all but heard about or read about in books.

  Smith has unwittingly taken advantage of a concept called an "Imaginary Mastermind."

  Napoleon Hill, author of *Think and Grow Rich*, first coined the term, "Mastermind." A Mastermind is a group that meets for the purpose of helping each other accomplish their goals. The group succeeds based upon the theory that more than one mind working together on a single objective creates a "Mastermind."

  Masterminds can be real or imaginary.

  In *Meet and Grow Rich*, the authors relate a story that Hill tells about a close friend who had an Imaginary Mastermind group made up of significant history figures, such as George Washington. The friend would visualize his group sitting around a conference table and having conversations. As a part of the group, eventually he realized that he'd incorporated some of their desired characteristics into his own personality. He credited his group as one of the keys to his success.[1]

---

[1] Meet and Grow Rich: How to Easily Create and Operate Your Own "Mastermind" Group for Health, Wealth, and More, Joe Vitale and Bill Hibbler, p.69 (Wiley 2006).

Building relationships early on can save you when you screw up

I don't plan on screwing up, you say. Good luck. Everybody makes mistakes. You don't want to make too many or major ones but they will happen.

But if you've built good will, that can help:

"There's this white partner and this white associate. The partner liked me. I took the work, didn't bother her, closed the deal, and the client was happy about it. The other associate and the partner did not get along at all. The associate screwed up, something minor. The partner went off on her, badmouthed her.

The partner and I worked on the same kind of deal. I screwed up. The partner said, 'No problem, we'll fix it, sweep it under the rug.' End of story.

The partner liked me. She didn't like the other associate. That could be the end of that associate's career at the firm. Word gets around, her hours drop. The view from the top is if you're not getting your hours, you're not a good lawyer.

It's a death spiral. The associate begins to question herself, gets angry, questions herself even more, has to get another job.

It all stems from whether you're liked or not."

—Anonymous Attorney

But specifically, how do you get mentors?

I mean, you don't just march boldly into their office, point at them and say, "You will be my mentor!" Or do you?

Strategy #10: Look for points of connection

Boayue-Gumbs first met Norman "Norm" Benson when she was looking for a job in Miami, FL. Simone, who lived in New York City and worked for Cravath, Swaine & Moore, planned to move to Miami because her husband had found a job there. Since Cravath did not have an office in Miami, she used the firm's alumnus network to find alumni working at large firms in Miami. She found Norm, who was a shareholder at Greenberg Traurig. The two met and hit it off. Now he serves as one of her mentors.

"Norm gives tidbits of advice. He has a daughter-in-law who is a Managing Director at Goldman Sachs, and she's also a mom. [Simone has two young children.] Part of my struggle is balancing work with children. He tells me constantly of his daughter-in-law. He has been helpful in that respect because I'm very hard on myself.

He left New York a little while ago. He has my best interests at heart. We have the same institutional history, culture. If I had a question, I have that comfort with him."

—Simone Boayue-Gumbs

Learning Points from Strategy #10:

- **Points of connection aren't always obvious.** One is obvious, the other less so. Simone and her mentor are alumni of the same firm and have a shared history of living and working in NYC. OK fine, but what else could she possibly have in common with a white, male senior partner? It turns out he has a daughter-in-law who shares the same challenges with Boayue-Gumb regarding work/life balance.

I heard this same point elsewhere:

"Men with professional daughters are often very good allies."

—Allegra Lawrence-Hardy

Strategy #11: Find ways to be of service to someone you'd like to have as a mentor

"We have an associate. She comes in my office, she asks me if I have anything I need help with, she asks if she can be on any cases with me. If I don't have anything that I need billable—a week ago she said I want to write an article with you. I said, 'Sure.'

And instead of then just waiting for me to come to her, she came back to me with an idea for the article. She did the research. She gave me a redwell with the articles.

I told her I'd look at the articles and follow up with me on Thursday. And sure enough Thursday morning I had an email from her saying, 'Is today a good time to talk? If not, let's talk tomorrow. And what time is convenient for you?' You know what I mean?

She's making it easy for me to mentor her. I told her, 'You're doing the right thing because I need to be writing articles. It's helpful for my career to write articles. But I don't really have the time.' Right now, her plate is not entirely full so she's using that time to do things like write articles.

I have to give a presentation on property rights on the Web for the ABA Litigation conference. And she's like, 'I'll help you prepare for that. I'll go do some research.'

So now I'm going to look out for her. She is putting in the effort in."

—Angela Payne James

Learning Points from Strategy #11:

- **Mentoring is a two-way street.** I'm guessing the associate Payne James described above is going to go far in her career. Stop waiting around for someone to mentor you and instead offer to be of service to them. As you can see from the above example, this partner you've put on a pedestal, who you think can't possibly need something from you, could use your help. Identify what you think their needs might be and see if you can fill them.

Strategy #12: Ask and ye shall receive

"I went to Frank Smith [Payne James practice group leader] and I said, 'I want you to be my mentor.' I said it just like that. I didn't pussyfoot around or say, 'Oh what should I do? How do I develop this mentoring relationship?' I was just like, 'Frank, be my mentor.' You're thinking how am I going to develop this relationship? Well just ask for the relationship.

Now at that point again I had done a good job, so Frank was like, kind of flattered that I saw him that way and wanted him to be my mentor."

—Angela Payne James

Learning Points from Strategy #12:

- **Go get 'em, Tiger.** Well, surprise, surprise, it looks like you *can* ask someone to be your mentor. You see, though, that Angela had put in the time <u>before</u> asking. She did quality work, she followed through, she built a relationship first. Then she asked.

Strategy #13: Let go of the fantasy that a mentor is a fairy godmother (or godfather)

"I think you have this vision that someone's going to come in your office and say, 'I see promise in you. Come with me.' And then just swoop you up and guide and direct your career and advise you and all of that. And it really doesn't work that way. It's really probably an 80/20 rule in terms of the mentee doing the work. Not being a pain in the rear, not sending me emails every five minutes but if they have the opening, following up."

—Angela Payne James

Learning Points from Strategy #13:

- **What that means is that you have to take responsibility.** This is not the time to be shy. It's not the time to say pitifully, "Well, this firm has a responsibility to mentor me, doesn't it? If they want me to succeed, they should want to provide me with someone who can guide me." Yes, they should. And I'll bet they do want to do that.

But it's not about them; it's about you taking responsibility, showing up. This is *your* career. No one is going to cultivate it better than you. Step up to the plate and take this challenge.

Strategy #14: Follow through, follow through, follow through

"You know how [when you meet someone who could be a potential mentor and they] say, 'Call me.' OK, did you call them? When you called them, did you have a specific thing you needed or a suggestion? You meet [people] at a conference and they say, 'Oh I'd love to have lunch with you.' And I say, 'Well here's my information. Just give me a call.' And you never hear from them. And that's a door open that wasn't taken."

—Angela Payne James

Learning Points from Strategy #14:

- **Seems obvious that you should follow through, doesn't it?** I can't tell you how many times I heard this complaint from partners that associates didn't do it though. Once given an opportunity, follow through with it. Not only is it a chance for you to build a relationship but also the converse is true—if you don't follow up, it may damage the relationship.

Strategy #15: Don't forget your peers as you're coming up, as well as those coming after you

"Women are tougher on other women. We can be a very strong, persuasive, powerful group if we work together. We are much more powerful as a unit than divided.

It's telling someone to go home because their son is sick, or their dog, or their mother. Help them out. Because it'll be reciprocated. Have a good strong core of people that support each other."

—Lisa Kobialka

"When I've complained [to myself] about not having a mentor, I've tried to serve as one. I've tried to be a mentor, make myself available informally and formally."

—Simone Boayue-Gumbs

Learning Points from Strategy #15:

- **Take care of each other.** It's so easy to get caught up in your own wants and needs. Remember that others have challenges too. How can you help? How can you be of service today? As Kobialka says, it will be reciprocated. Not to mention you're building that strong core of people who support each other. How awesome is that?

- **Don't forget to do your part and mentor others.** What a brilliant strategy Boayue-Gumbs has hit upon! Whenever you complain about what you don't have, go out and serve. That's good advice for life actually. "But I'm a first year!" you argue. Mentor a law school student or pre-law college student. "I'm only in my second, third, fourth year!" you say. Recall what Angela said in Strategy #7 above: Some of the folks who mentored her are now peers because they're so close in years, but when she was a first year, they were incredibly helpful because they knew more than she did.

An Ode to Mentors

If for some bizarre reason you're still not sold on the importance of having mentors, I'm going to give you a glimpse of just how powerful these relationships can be.

Rhonda Adams Medina is Senior Vice President, Business and Legal Affairs, Deputy General Counsel, Nickelodeon/MTV Networks Kids and Family Group in New York City. Here's what Adams Medina had to say when I asked her who her mentors were and how they've helped:

Charles Ogletree, professor at Harvard Law School. *"He has been to me, next to my parents, the most influential moral compass I've had in my career. I look at what he's done with his legal education and feel as if he has answered a higher calling."*

Spike Lee, filmmaker, director, producer, writer. *"Spike has opened the doors for so many people in entertainment. I met Spike at Harvard. I was in his class as a student. I did a year as his teaching assistant. He took an interest in me based upon my performance in his class. I asked him, 'Can I get a job in your organization?' I asked him literally a few days before he left. He responded immediately and positively.*

He put me in touch with people in the entertainment field. People return your calls when you say, 'Spike Lee told me to call you.' He had nothing to gain because I was quite the powerless student."

Lisa Davis, Partner, Frankfurt Kurnit Klein & Selz PC. *"We naturally gravitated toward one another. Lisa was Spike's attorney, and he introduced us. When a job came up at her firm, she suggested that I interview. She took ownership over my career when I got there."*

40

Andra Shapiro, Executive Vice President, Business Affairs and General Counsel, Nickelodeon. *"I wouldn't have been here for twelve years if I didn't have an extraordinary relationship with Andra. She's a very generous boss—generous with her time, with her contacts, with her knowledge. She's a fantastic person to learn from and work with and she has championed my career."*—Rhonda Adams Medina

Wow. May you be equally blessed with mentors just like these.

CHAPTER 5

Relationships with Clients

"Good fortune is what happens when opportunity meets with planning."

—Thomas Edison

When you start, the easiest thing you can do in the client department is to build relationships with the firm's current clients. Let's look at how you do that.

Strategy #1: Make a connection with individuals

"We do a lot of work for one company and so we have a couple of repeat players. I have lunch with the V.P. We are both professional women with kids. We have that in common. Same with another. You connect to people on a person-to-person level.

With those two, we talk so often and email, you feel like they're friends of yours."

—Simone Boayue-Gumbs

"I try to have personal relationships with clients. Family is important to me. I have four children. I want people to know that. I want to know about their children. There's a lot more loyalty when a face and personality are connected with legal work. It makes it more fun."

—Elizabeth Reza

Learning Points from Strategy #1:

- **Search for those points of connection as if they are buried treasure.** That's what they're worth after all. "Well I don't have kids," you say. OK, kids are not the only point of connection for humans. Find out their likes, dislikes, interests, hobbies, desires, challenges. And, yes, this is a long-term strategy. You can't pull out a clipboard with your questions, interview the client, and get to this stuff. Boayue-Gumbs' firm does a lot of work for this client, so that means she has spent a lot of time with these people. This is a relationship that she has built over the long-term.

Strategy #2: Be responsive to clients

"So long as you're servicing people and you're available to them, there's no need for ill will."

—Simone Boayue-Gumbs

Learning Points from Strategy #2:

- **Be available.** If that isn't one of the Golden Rules, I don't know what is. And here's a strategy you can use from Day One of your career that will serve you incredibly well. There is nothing that can turn a relationship sour more quickly than not keeping your commitments and being inaccessible. And once that trust is broken, here comes that ill will Boayue-Gumbs is talking about. And trust me, you don't want to be the cause of ill will.

Strategy #3: Don't overlook your peers at the client's office . . . or your existing network

"The younger you are, the more you should be establishing relationships with your peers at the client's. Social, if possible. That young analyst at the investment bank is getting hazed just like you are. Go for drinks, stay in contact. They grow up quickly and end up in positions of influence.

Stay connected to people. I had a meeting in New York recently with a guy I carpooled with in elementary school. When I first moved to New York, he was a baby broker at an investment bank. Now he's the managing director of a global hedge fund with two billion dollars. I reconnected with him through his sister on Facebook.

After the meeting with him, I was walking down the street and I passed [this guy from college.] He hands me his card; he's managing partner of an equity fund.

You should be cultivating and growing your network, doing favors for people. All that good will come back.

I get calls out of the blue six or seven years later. A woman I knew in law school was a summer associate and junior associate at our Chicago office. She left to start a real estate business. She has a deal and asked me if I could look at the documents.

Never underestimate people. You may look around at your friends today and say they're chumps. Never underestimate the power of time."

—Sulee Clay

Learning Points from Strategy #3:

- **Cultivate and grow your network.** In that one story, Clay referred to peers at the client's, an elementary school classmate, a college classmate, and a law school classmate. If you think your network is small, you're not taking into account the hundreds of people you've already encountered in your life up until now.
- **Never underestimate the power of time.** As Clay says, folks your age may not impress you right now (after all, you knew them when they were chugging beers at a dorm party) but give them a few years, they could very well be in high-powered positions and in a position to send you some lucrative matters—as long as you stay in touch.

Developing and maintaining relationships with the firm's current clients is a critical step in your advancement at the firm. Clients who think that you do excellent work and enjoy working with you not only work with you on current matters, but also will bring you new matters. That's new billable work for the firm, and the firm is getting it because of your efforts. That type of business development is rewarded.

At a certain point in your career, you're ready for the next step though: strategies for cultivating new clients.

The Mystery of Getting New Clients

"It is certainly huge at this stage of your career when you want to continue to succeed. Because at a certain point doing a great job and being really smart and working really hard . . . that's going to be a given. And there's this next additional piece of, are you really developing substantial business.

Now, at most large law firms, there is still a place for the person who is profitable because they do great work and they do a lot of it even at the partner level. But certainly law firm businesses have evolved to where the business development piece is big and some places that's what they want. And it's not enough to be able to run the case and do the great job and all of that.

My personal view is, given what we do [IP Litigation], and given the size of the cases, it is a little bit harder I believe to bring in those kind of

45

giant cases without the grey hair factor. Because these are not cases you are going to get because you're having a cocktail at the ABA reception.

Now, ultimately, it's still important to have these relationships and make these relationships. And I do. I get out and I speak and I go to these things and try to network with people and build relationships.

But for this type of litigation, it's really going to boil down to expertise and experience. That's for bringing in the new client as a big patent litigation client.

Business development is a combination of all of your effort and then there's a factor that's just complete luck and timing. And frankly that often is the bigger factor.

You can do all the things 'they' tell you to do. You can go to every event and know your client's business and choose and be an expert at what you do. But it just may be that that company doesn't ever have that opportunity in what you're doing with the person that you know who has the power to give you that work. It just may not ever work out from a timing, luck, and opportunity standpoint despite the fact that you have done everything in the world that you can possibly do.

On the other hand, you may get the lucky random phone call because you met somebody once. We just met with a client who we were just doing a get-to-know-you type thing with and they happened to mention some patent problem. And it happened to be that we were already involved with that patent in other litigation and now we have this great opportunity.

*But that was fairly random. You know, you be prepared when the opportunity comes but it really—**it's a combination of being prepared and having some good luck and timing on your side.***

That can be frustrating because in my view there isn't this secret to success where if you do this combination of things every single time that's going to result in getting some huge patent case."

—Angela Payne James

I simply had to include this quote because it encapsulates all that's practical and magical about the process of bringing in new clients.

Now let's look at some individual strategies.

Strategy # 5: Build your reputation as a thoughtful, hard worker early on—even earlier than you can imagine

Payne James reeled in a large client at a relatively early stage in her career. She was a fourth-year associate. I asked her how in the world that happened.

46

"That came about because of my law-school roommate. [After law school, Angela's roommate joined a company as in-house counsel. When the opportunity to hire outside counsel appeared, she thought of Angela.] And [my roommate said], 'Look, I know you will take care of this and I know you will make sure that it's done properly.' Her CEO had great confidence in her and basically said, 'You go get who you want' and then [my friend] brought it to me. And then that's how it happened.

It ended up being . . . this huge thing. That helped build a foundation for my career and my reputation. And really that was from [my friend] having confidence in me from our law school days."

—Angela Payne James

Learning Points from Strategy #5:

- **Someone's always watching.** Sounds creepier than it is. I just mean that it doesn't hurt to look at your actions and words in the light of, "If what I'm saying/doing was splashed in the headlines of the local newspaper, would I be OK with that?"

  Does that mean that you're *never* allowed to cut loose? No, it's not that. But I'd rather have the reputation in law school of being a conscientious student than the party girl on balance. The latter is not going to stand you in good stead once you graduate.

Strategy #6: Inherit them

Tandy's story about how she developed her book of business is interesting:

"I did it the old-fashioned way. I inherited them. [laughs] I don't have nearly the book of business as my counterparts my age. Which is a function of the type of work I do but also that I'm not practicing full-time [due to her position as Diversity Chair for the firm]. But most of what I do I have inherited from my mentor who retired the same year that I made partner."

—Lovita Tandy

Learning Points from Strategy #6:

- **Cross your fingers?** Not exactly. You should be able to intuit this one because this won't be the first time I've said it: <u>Do quality work</u>. The only way you acquire a retiring partner's book of business is to do an excellent job so that you can make partner and take over his work. Don't knock it if you haven't tried it.

47

Strategy #7: If you don't ask, you won't get

"The day I made partner, I put on my "man hat"—asking, what would white boys do?" Number one: I should be getting credit for clients we service. Number two: I'm interested in making equity partner. I wanted folks to know that for me [making partner] was not the end-all, be-all.

I went to [this senior partner with whom I had been servicing a client] and asked for credit. He said, 'No one's ever demanded credit from me.' I felt I deserved that; he refused. He told me to talk to him next year. On January 2nd the following year—'Here I am.' He said OK.

You're not going to get [credit] necessarily the first time you ask. If you don't ask, you don't get it. If you don't ask, you're a fool. They'd [white men] ask.

It's learning how to play the game."

—Sulee Clay

Learning Points from Strategy #7:

- **Put on your "man" hat.** A funny expression perhaps, but an apt analogy that describes the sense of entitlement that white men in the U.S. possess that allows them to take advantage of opportunities we often miss. Since often women of color are not raised this way, and, yet, they too are entitled to the same benefits, they have to imagine what it would be like to be in the shoes of a white male. By doing so, you are guaranteeing that you will be able to see the opportunities that are available to you and take advantage of them.
- **Be persistent.** As Clay mentioned, you may not get what you asked for the first time around but "No" now does not mean "No" forever. Be persistent, ask again, *especially* when a partner advises you that that's what you should do, as Clay mentioned in her story above.
- **Get help from your mentors.** How did Clay know how to make these types of demands? One of her mentors told her how! In Strategy #9, Chapter 4, Clay discussed how one of her mentors outside of the firm, a black woman partner, helped her to prepare for these conversations. This is yet another reason why mentors are so important.

Strategy #8: Here's your chance to sit at the feet of a master rainmaker

Lawrence-Hardy treats business development as a discipline. When I heard her describe her plan, I got chills, both because it's so meticulous,

48

it's scary, and because it clearly explains why she's so good at business development. This quote is going to be another long one, but I promise you it is well worth it.

> *"**Learn your craft very well.** It's about focusing on your craft. Learning to be the best lawyer you can be. That sometimes means working with unpleasant people because they have a skill set you need.*
>
> *In terms of business development, it became clear to me early on and frankly it was from NALP, ABA studies that black partners do not tend to inherit clients statistically speaking.*
>
> ***I treated it like a discipline.** I took business development classes. I got training at the New Partner Institute. I was the only partner [my year] who asked.*
>
> *Others took for granted they'd get things. I never did. Now you see what's been going on over the last 18 months [the economic downturn]. God bless me for making me a black woman. The service partners don't have any clients. I've never had that luxury.*
>
> *It was clear I had to develop relationships. I really studied it. I went to all-day workshops on business development. **It became my biggest strength.** I read sales books. For example, I read I was much more likely to make sales in a navy suit versus a tan suit. I learned about kinesthetic learners versus auditory learners. I tried to learn psychology. I will read sales books for anybody selling anything. I go to the library to borrow books. I go to every course.*
>
> *I'm very disciplined. I have a weekly system of business development. I do it every day. **I treat it as if it's as important as client matters.***
>
> *Just to give you an example: **I do a weekly business development plan.** I develop a plan that contains internal marketing, brand building, prospective client marketing, and current client marketing. In each area I do something each week. I write an article, I go to lunch, I write a thank-you note. On Wednesdays my accountability partner and I talk at 8:00 a.m. We check in with one another. On Friday we finish our reports and exchange them.*
>
> *I'm doing a program called Women Rainmakers. When the trainer asked us to raise our hand if we've done more than one million dollars in business, I was the only one who raised my hand."*

—Allegra Lawrence-Hardy

Learning Points from Strategy #8:

- **Treat business development like a discipline.** To do that, it means you have to study. Read every book you can find on business development, sales, marketing, branding—whether they relate to the practice of law or not. You can learn from anyone who is a master at sales and marketing.

- **Make business development a priority.** Imitate Lawrence-Hardy and learn to treat business development as if it's as important as your client matters. Because it is.
- **Create a weekly business development plan.** And follow through. Lawrence-Hardy says she works on her plan every day. The steps don't have to be complicated. Little steps that you take every day add up to a lot once the 365 days of the year have passed. It's when you try to create something massive and pro-crastinate, because it's so massive, that time slips away and next thing you know it's another year and you've done nothing.
- **Create accountability.** As disciplined and committed as Lawrence-Hardy is, she doesn't just rely on herself. She creates accountability by having a partner. They talk twice a week, once in the middle of the week to stay on track, and once at the end of the week to exchange plans and talk about what they've accomplished and what's ahead.
- **Take advantage of learning opportunities.** Make opportunities if you have to. Lawrence-Hardy *asked* to attend the New Partner Institute. Don't assume the firm is going to take charge of your training. Be aware of what's available and be persistent about asking to attend. Lawrence-Hardy has attended numerous courses and programs. She still does, even at her level of success, because you can *always* learn more. Take the one-day programs, take the three-day programs, the week-long programs, the ongoing programs that provide coaching and training and accountability.
- **Make business development your biggest strength.** How do you do this? By making it a priority, learning everything you can, and taking action. Practice, practice, practice.

Think of all you can do, what you can accomplish if you become a rainmaker! For Lawrence-Hardy, practicing law at a Big Firm is about much more than just being one of the first black women partners at her firm (although, of course, that is a tremendous accomplishment in and of itself). But she has much larger aspirations. To her, being a woman of color practicing law at a Big Firm is about changing the face of the legal profession. She wants to see more and more of us there with her.

One of her favorite quotes, that she keeps displayed in her office, is *"Be the change you want to see."*—Gandhi.

How does she do that? It's all about the book of business.

"To be the change, you have to have a book of business. You have to have the ability to get people assigned to projects and to protect people. The day I crossed one million dollars things changed. The day I crossed two million dollars things changed again."

—Allegra Lawrence-Hardy

CHAPTER 6

I Can't Be Being Discriminated Against, Can I?

"Diversity—it is not an obligation—it is an opportunity."

—Malcolm Forbes

I've been a very fortunate girl. I can remember experiencing only one incident of overt racism in my lifetime. I proudly served as a Safety Patrol monitor in elementary school. I stopped a little girl who was cutting across the grass to tell her to use the sidewalk and she said, "Get your dirty black hand off me." Amazing, right? And this wasn't that long ago. This incident occurred in the late '70's. [If you're concerned if she got away with it, she didn't. I went to a teacher, he went to her parents, and they all ended up apologizing.]

Racism in my life has typically been more subtle. As a result, my parents, who unfortunately had to live through segregation, have fought a lot of battles for me, especially in my formative years at school, that I didn't always see. They could sniff out when teachers weren't giving me the proper grades or honors or trying to mess with my little impressionable mind because of my race. They could tell when I was questioning my worth thanks to nasty, insidious comments made by teachers or students (such as, "She's such a nice little black girl") and were quick to point out to me that I was just as smart, if not smarter, than the white kids in my class.

The racial stuff I remember has to do with being one of very few black kids in my school. There were 69 in my class and only three of us were black. I remember when we reached the age where girls started noticing boys and vice versa. When they started sending each other notes, asking each other to dance at the school dance, "going steady." What I remember most vividly is everyone encouraging me to go out with one of the two black boys in our class. There was nothing wrong with those boys but why was there this unspoken rule that I couldn't date one of the white guys?

Or when I got into Harvard early action and a classmate sniffed, "Well you got in because of affirmative action." Ouch. But darn it, do you know at the time I secretly wondered if she was right?

That's how dangerous insidious racism is. It's nothing you can necessarily point to and say, "Ah ha! Racism!" You can't quite put your finger on it. All you know is that it doesn't feel quite right and you're not sure if there's anything you can do about it. Or that there's anything you *want* to do about it. Who wants to be known as the person who's always playing the "race card?"

As one associate told me:

"When I joined my firm, at first I just kept my head down, you know, getting the work done. Everybody was really nice too so it seemed to be working out fine. But after a year I looked up and realized that all of the other associates, who were white, had their own clients. They hadn't brought them into the firm but somehow had ended up assigned as the Client Contact. But I didn't have one. I asked the partner about it at my review and he just shrugged it off. He said it was just the way things worked, over time I'd probably get one of my own, not to worry about it. But it never "just happened" like he said it would.

Now I'm just as smart as those people. I went to a top five law school and most of the rest of them didn't. They were local yokels. And I'm just as good at my work. I can only conclude that for some reason the "black girl" was deemed not capable of managing a client.

But what could I do? It wasn't explicit. Nobody ever said anything like that. It was so frustrating."

—Anonymous Attorney

Or:

"They commented on my hair. They mistake me for the fax person. It's mostly very subtle; work assignments, who gets plugged into work opportunities."

—Anonymous Attorney

Or:

> *"I started to see that the partners were treating the associate who was a white man differently. He'd gone to the same college as the team leader. I'd look at his work and mine. Not only were they about the same but sometimes mine was better. I once submitted my work to a partner with [that] associate's name on it and got a different reaction."*

—Anonymous Attorney

So what *can* you do? I'm not going to act like you can just wave a magic wand and poof! this kind of stuff will be resolved. Unfortunately, there aren't necessarily easy solutions. Let's see what our illustrious panel of partners has to say.

Strategy #1: Check in with someone in charge

> *"There was a situation sort of early on. Where I was sent to do a document review at another firm. And they didn't realize I was a lawyer. And it caused some sort of problems because I think [the firm] had promised to send a lawyer. . . . And David Onorato [former partner at King & Spalding] went off. And they did not realize that I was a lawyer and they later did. He just went off, made them apologize to me."*

—Lovita Tandy

> *"[A senior white male partner once chided me, saying] 'What I or anyone in your parents' generation would [chastise you for is] working when you have a child and don't have to.' How did he know whether I didn't have to work? I told him, 'My mom was a lawyer and she worked when we were kids. She wouldn't agree with you.'*
>
> *I called the Managing Partner. I went to his office and that thing you dread happening happened. I started bawling. I had this conversation with him and he was like 'Oh my God!' He brings out his box of tissues. He was delightful and supportive and talked to the [offending] partner and dealt with it.*
>
> *I'm so glad I did. Otherwise I would have stewed and been miserable."*

—Anonymous Attorney

Learning Points from Strategy #1:

- **Don't go it alone.** You don't have to. If you're working with good people (remember those mentors), they are there to help you. Tell them what's going on and let them help you sort it out. Some of the partners (including Managing Partners) are very sensitive to these kinds of issues:

55

"Another woman partner and I watch the hours. We noticed the white boys were getting more hours. We had to step in. The senior white boys had gotten comfortable, they gravitated toward three white boys. Totally unconscious. They would never consider themselves racist. The white associates were doing what they needed to do. We intervened. Told the partners they need to be mindful of being more inclusive."

—Anonymous Attorney

- **Don't forget your Diversity Committee.** Lovita Tandy, who chairs the Atlanta chapter of King & Spalding's Diversity Committee, tells me that she has heard a lot of sob stories. What does that tell me? She's the go-to person for this kind of stuff. If you've got a Diversity Committee, take advantage! If you don't have one, lobby for one.

Strategy #2: Check in with your peers

"There were incidents where you know my first year I was convinced that I was being discriminated against, absolutely convinced because there was no other reason that I could understand why this associate, this senior associate, was treating me so poorly. He would yell, he would talk down to me, he was very sarcastic. There were times where he tried to throw me under the bus. I mean, I had not been here a month and he tried to throw me under the bus and Scott Blews [former associate at King & Spalding] pulled me out. And in my mind either [the senior associate] was discriminating against me or I was really so stupid that Harvard, Duke, and King & Spalding had all made errors. High school had to take me but everybody else screwed up, ok?

And I believed that in my heart of hearts until about November of my second year when the white male first year who was working for him came into my office and was like, 'What is with this asshole?' "

—Lovita Tandy

Learning Points from Strategy #2:

- **Anybody else think this guy's a jerk?** Looks like Tandy could have saved herself some grief if she'd asked around. Not much grief, mind you, since the senior associate was still going to drive her crazy. But at least she would have known it wasn't because he was racist. Look, you've got more than enough on your plate with work, getting to understand the culture and politics, and trying to have a little bit of a life. That extra burden of thinking someone is discriminating against you is enough to tip the balance into making the situation unbearable.

- **So maybe sometimes it *isn't* racism.** Hard to tell sometimes, sure. All you can do in these types of situations, where nothing direct has been said or done, is take a cool, hard look at them. Again, this is where pulling in someone with more experience can be helpful.

Strategy #3: Let your talent speak for you

"I went to Mississippi to try a case. I was representing the biggest defendant. Someone asked me if I was the court reporter. I announced, 'I'm here for the biggest defendant.' The judge asked, 'Oh. Is there another lawyer with you?' You could tell he was thinking, 'What's a black girl doing here?'

I won the case.

I called Peter Anderson [partner at Sutherland, Asbill & Brennan]. I told him I won the motion but it was a horrible day. He told me, 'Hang up and get out of there as fast as you can.' "

—Allegra Lawrence-Hardy

Learning Points from Strategy #3:

- **Say what they want, they can't take your accomplishments away from you.** No matter what they say, they can't take those away from you. You show them who you are by what you do, how you perform. Remember that when the jerks are getting you down.

Strategy #4: Let the situation dictate your approach

"[Situations] more fall into the category [of discriminatory] by virtue of me being a woman. I'm half Asian. So people don't necessarily look at me and say, 'She's a minority.'

In litigation, especially IP, it's largely dominated by men. You definitely experience things; they can be nuanced. You get overlooked, ignored. They refer to you as 'sweetie.'

I've had to take a different approach in every situation. [If it's unintentional], I let them know in a joking way. If it's intentional, I handle it differently.

No man wants to be dressed down by a woman. It can be a very powerful thing if you're smart about it.

I was taking the deposition of a CEO of a publicly traded company. When I walked in, the lawyers were all male. The court reporter was a female. The CEO introduced himself to everyone but me.

57

I introduced myself. I said, 'You're here because I'm going to be taking your deposition.' He was so mortified by what he'd done. As we went through the deposition, he gave me everything I wanted. He went above and beyond.

You have to have the right perspective on it. Make sure you understand what the intent is. If it's unintentional, it's just plain stupid. Everybody does stupid things, all of us. You have to make allowances.

If it's intentional, that's a very different thing."

—Lisa Kobialka

Learning Points from Strategy #4:

- **Understand intent.** As Kobialka points out, intent determines the type of strategy she uses to handle discriminatory situations. Save your hammer for those times when someone is intentionally trying to discriminate against you.
- **Perceptions exist.** Stereotypes exist. We can rail against them or we can just accept that it's so, be aware of them, and counter them as necessary.

Strategy #5: Don't sweat the small stuff

"It's that subtle shocked look. Or I walk into a room and the white man who is junior to me is the one people start talking to. So what? I have to brush that off. It's not a big deal. You're not going to get anywhere in [the business world] if someone gives you a look you don't like."

—Anonymous Attorney

"Generally speaking I look younger. When I started, people would ask, 'How old are you? How many years have you practiced? How much experience do you have?' With males who are seven years junior to me, that's not a question clients would ask. I recognize it and understand it and have to put my best foot forward. I really have to make sure they understand I know what I'm doing. I have to work harder than white males with a little gray hair who are junior to me."

—Lisa Kobialka

Learning Points from Strategy #5:

- **Save your energy for the big battles.** Even if they mistake you for the junior person, they'll quickly realize that they're wrong. Plus, admit it: you might get a perverse sense of satisfaction from the looks on their faces when they realize they've made a mistake.

Is it racism . . . or not?

"When I was a very junior associate, probably a first year, I was on a case with an older white male. And we were preparing for trial. The partner said something like 'Well you might get to get some stand-up experience at trial depending on what the jury looks like.' And when he first said it, I was sort of like, 'OK that makes perfect sense.' [laughs]

And then I thought about it and I was like, 'Well wait, what does that mean?' I think he probably meant, if there's a lot of women or a lot of African-Americans on the jury, I might be more inclined to have you stand up and do something.

But I didn't really immediately recognize it that way. As a first year I think I was thinking, 'OK I think he means let's see how things shake out in the case and we'll see what happens and then we'll decide.' I think later, having reflected on it, it may have meant something different.

And so at the time you know I didn't do anything about it because I don't know that I perceived it as being discriminatory at the time.

And I don't think he meant it that way. I think it just reflected what we see sometimes—it wasn't that he was holding me back from an opportunity. I think he felt that OK here was an opportunity that you might not get, that you might not otherwise have if I perceive that your gender or your race might have a benefit for the case.

And you know that's not uncommon at all in the legal world, you know, and it's not uncommon from clients too. Clients, if they're litigating in a particular district or location, might want to have a more diverse team. And that's not necessarily a bad thing.

But does that mean that the converse is true? If you don't perceive a particular benefit from my race or gender, am I then not going to get the opportunity?

And that's where I think it becomes clearly problematic and more what we might call discriminatory."

—Anonymous Attorney

Some of it, you just can't control

"When I made partner, I was the only woman and the only person of color. My boyfriend said, 'They are not going to let a black girl make partner when [some of the] white boys didn't.' When I got to work the next day, they were redoing the count. All . . . of us made partner. I say to those . . . guys [who didn't make it at first], 'Aren't you lucky you came up with a black girl!'

[Before the recount] people kept coming by my office saying things to me: 'Aren't you upset so-and-so didn't make partner (because of his wife and kids)?' What does that have to do with me?"—Anonymous Attorney

"Every time there's a compensation cycle, I get a raise in compensation. Despite the fact that I'm collecting a lot of money each year, [others think that] my managing partner is paying me that because I'm black. He came to me and said, 'Others are taking issue with your compensation because you're so young.' It's not because I'm young. It's because I'm young, a woman, and black.

I lose friends every compensation cycle."

—Anonymous Attorney

What's all this fuss about diversity anyway?

Sure, we get that for our own sakes diversity is a good thing. We also understand that it's the "right" thing to do, the ethical approach. But is there more to it than that?

I thought I'd check in with an expert on this topic, thinking that if we understand all of the reasons why diversity is important, it'll give you just a little more oomph, that extra something you need to keep you striving for success at the Big Firm.

Diversity consultant, Vernā Myers, provided a thought-provoking and inspirational response when I asked her: what is the power of diversity?

"As lawyers we are in such a narrow worldview as to how to solve problems, predict issues, manage people.

If you can get people together from different perspectives and backgrounds and they respect each other (because that's important) and you can put them on a problem, there is really no end to what you can produce, solve, create.

That's the thing I feel even the most excellent firms have not tapped: the power that comes from unleashing difference. We are very much into playing down differences, being homogenized.

Even if I look at these [excellent] firms, you look at their management. [I want to ask,] 'You feel safe with having these replicas all sitting around discussing the future of the firm? You don't want a young person on your management committee? You don't want several women? You don't want different languages, different socioeconomic groups? You really think this is best? I know it's working for you.' [But] I don't think we have any idea what best could look like.

It would be so great if we could learn to grow different. Welcoming difference. Not just inviting people in to be the same. Asking them to challenge the model—what do we need to change, what are we doing well, what other voices do we need, how could we look different?

They can't do this because for a lot of people this is an intellectual idea. For others, they've experienced the power. They say, 'Dang, I could have never thought of that!' It's not because they're not bright. It's because they come from another place.

If you live in a narrow world where you're at the top, you don't always have the experience of being wowed by someone else's point of view."

—Vernā Myers, JD, Principal, Vernā Myers Consulting Group

CHAPTER 7

Assimilate or Not?

"Say it loud! I'm black, I'm proud!"

—James Brown

How do your race and ethnicity come into play in the workplace? And how do you want them to come into play?

The *Visible Invisibility* study conducted by the Commission on Women in the Profession stated:

"Women of color in the survey and focus groups felt that they could not 'be themselves'; they downplayed and homogenized their gender and racial/ethnic identities. . . . The effort to minimize the impact of their physical differences was stressful to many women of color, an added burden to the long hours and hard work demanded by their firm."[1]

Here's how partners see it:

"This is really who I am. I've grown up in an integrated situation my entire life. My personality is who I am. I don't feel like I'm letting go of a burden when I get home—'Phwew, I can be myself.'

I probably do tolerate things others would not. It's not blatant. But in my gut, I know it's probably not appropriate.

My husband says that I make people feel comfortable. He says, 'You're very open. You make people feel really comfortable and sometimes they cross the line.'

---

[1] Visible Invisibility: Women of Color in Law Firms (American Bar Association Commission on Women of Color in the Profession), p. xii

Even at work people say, 'You're an apologist. You want everybody to get along.' I don't want a lot of conflict. I'm very competitive though. But I root for the underdog. I don't feel like you advance by stepping on other people.

There was plenty of time I went to stuff I didn't want to go to—Chastain Park concerts with Neil Sedaka, LTO. I try to hum along. I didn't want to be the first to dance though."

[I jumped into the interview here to say: "I agree with that. It's definitely a no-no to be the first one dancing if you're the minority. Also, I typically don't eat fried chicken, especially chicken wings, in front of white people because it's a terrible stereotype associated with us."]

"No chicken, no watermelon. [laughs]"

—Nicole Pierre, J.D., Corporate Public Affairs Manager, UPS, Washington, D.C.

"I don't hide the fact that I'm Caribbean. It'll come up. I identify with my West Indian heritage but I don't dress in any particular way. I dress as a professional. I don't think I'm doing anything per se to 'fit in.' My goal is to be a professional first. I came from JP Morgan. That was my way of approaching it. I never felt the need to change who I am to fit in."

—Charmaine Slack

"You don't sound black"

"Sean Carter, an HLS graduate who calls himself a 'Humorist at Law,' is hilarious. He said that all black lawyers have a 'white voice.' It's the voice we use at work. [laughs] I knew I was using that voice when a client called with questions and starts going on about how lazy blacks are. I let him finish his tirade, gave him employment advice, and scheduled a meeting. I went out there, and I was like, 'Here I am.' The look on his face was totally worth it."

—Allegra Lawrence-Hardy

African American women and their hair

Let's take what appears to be a simple issue: your hair. For African American women, it's not always such a simple issue. Take braids. Would you wear them at work or would you not? Is this even a question?

It was for me. I remember when I decided to wear braids—first as a summer intern at a television station in my hometown, Savannah, GA, when I was a college student (early 90's), and then as an associate at a boutique law firm in Atlanta, GA (early 2000). My parents were concerned that I might lose my job. As a result of my braids.

As a college student, I was defiant. I didn't care. (Actually, I cared but I was crossing my fingers, hoping my parents were wrong.) As it turns out, the television station didn't have a problem with it.

It mattered a bit more to me when I was an associate at a boutique law firm, Mazursky & Dunaway LLP (now Mazursky Constantine, LLC). This was my career and a six-figure salary we were talking about here. So I decided to take charge. I got the braids. But then I went to name partner, Don Mazursky, and said, "My parents are worried that I'll lose my job since I got braids. Will I?" (Needless to say, I obviously had a very good relationship with Mazursky since I felt so bold as to ask such a direct question.)

He laughed and promptly wrote me a note. It read, "I promise that I will not fire Monica due to her multiple, multiple braids." He signed and dated it. My parents were relieved. (And probably also a bit frightened at the audacity of their daughter.)

Some of you reading this passage may be thinking, what's the big deal? It's just hair. At my firm, women wear braids, cornrows, or natural hairstyles. It's not a big deal.

"I have had braids here. I've had braids I think two or three times for stretches. No issue whatsoever. I don't think I even had the thought, is this going to be a problem. Because, you know, there have been other women here with braids. And that again is a function of we've had a decent number of people [of color]. So you're not the only one.

So when you're the only one or one of two, you probably feel like [when you change] your hairstyle, there's more attention paid. And there probably is because you are the only one or two. But I've never had that problem here.

And frankly I think it's because we are in Atlanta. Atlanta has a large percentage of African American professionals. People are not unaccustomed to different hairstyles. I mean, Shirley Franklin is our mayor. She wears her hair a lot of different styles. The most popular [television news] broadcaster is Monica Kaufman who also changes her hair all the time.

So you know I never got the feeling that people here thought differently about hairstyles when it came to women because I think they've seen it."

—Angela Payne James

Others of you may be shaking your head. There's no way, you say. My firm is way too conservative for that. Or, not in my town.

65

"My firm was very conservative. In the Bible Belt. There was the good ol' boy syndrome throughout the firm and the state. When I interviewed I had very long straight hair. [During my interview] I [met] with one of the black associates who had braids. I thought that was very interesting. She told me that the firm is a very conservative firm in a very conservative place but that once you're in, they're not going to say anything.

But for the majority of the time I was always cognizant of keeping my hair a certain way."

—Anonymous Attorney

That can be the case whether it's the Bible Belt or the ultra-cosmopolitan New York City. As one partner who grew up in a prestigious New York law firm said, *"I'm not a big braid person but I probably wouldn't have done it anyway. [Although] firms are probably more accepting of different hairstyles than ten years ago."*

—Anonymous Attorney

When I asked one attorney if there were similar issues for her as an Asian-American woman, she joked, *"What am I going to do? It's not like I'm going to wear traditional Chinese garb in the office. They're not going to take me seriously if I wear a long, tight dress with a slit up one side."*

—Anonymous Attorney

But how about stereotypes?

Stereotypes

Unfortunately, minorities are forever fighting against stereotypes. I've found that typically in settings where the majority race is, well, the majority, a lot of them have not had extensive contact with members of minority races. As a result, they may unwittingly buy into stereotypes of minorities. A lot of the women I talked to feel compelled to be proactive in their efforts to provide counter examples to those stereotypes.

"Because there's such a stereotype of Asian-American women being submissive, I try to be more aggressive. Maybe it's partially because I'm from Texas and because I have small hands, but I have a firm handshake. People comment about it all the time. I need to show I have some power. I'm 5'1," Asian American, and hopefully I still look young. [laughs]"

—Bettina Yip, General Attorney, AT&T, Atlanta, GA

Note: As of the time this book went to print, Yip had left AT&T to be-come Associate General Counsel for Labor & Employment at Del Monte Foods in San Francisco, CA.

Here's another example:

Well, the choice I made early on was that I did not want to be stereotyped as sort of the "big, black, angry woman." That I am. [laughs] And so I think I made my natural personality—I made myself very, very reserved professionally. And there were [only] a couple of people who I really felt like I could let go a little bit more with.

And I don't do that anymore. But I did it for a long time. And it was huge emotional drain.

—Lovita Tandy

Yip's comment when I shared the above story above with her: *"For me being Asian-American, I'd much rather be perceived as an angry Asian-Amer-ican woman than a passive Asian-American woman."*—Bettina Yip

As an African-American I'm always worried about being perceived as lazy or not smart. I can't count the number of times my mom had to go to bat for us at school because of a racial stereotype that black chil-dren aren't as smart as white children. (It wasn't that long ago, you know, that some scientists tried to prove that our brains were different and therefore, inferior.)

Asian-Americans have to fight the opposite implication, that they *are* smart. Huh? Why would you fight that?

"The stereotype is that Asians are smart. But it's math and science. But I wanted to prove that I was just as smart at English and History. I won awards because I felt I had to prove that even though I look the way I do, my English is just as good and I can get your history.

I'm not in math and science, so I have to prove myself competent."

—Bettina Yip

Asian-American women also have to fight against their youthful looks:

"Remember you're in a service industry. Who you represent. What is it they're looking for? If you're an Asian American you're going to look very young. If you wear your hair in ponytails all the time, do you think that a client is going to look at you and want you as counsel in a high-stakes litigation for millions of dollars?"

—Lisa Kobialka

Wearing the navy suit

I remember my first handful of interviews at the firm for summer clerk-ships. I wore the same navy suit every time. I'd been advised by people I trusted that interviewing was not a time for individuality. Especially for black folks. It was so boring.

"I did a lot of that when I was younger [worrying about assimilating]. I don't have the energy now to wear the mask. I have an O.V. Brantley quilt with black women [on it] in my office.

I had a ton of pinstriped suits. I was so careful. I'd wear charcoal all day. That's not me.

Now I wear animal print and red. It makes me happy. I have six red suits. I love a red suit. I like animal print. I enjoy more being me.

It became more painful to stay in the shell than to get out.

In fact, I'm thinking about getting braids. If I had the face for it, I'd wear a natural."

—Allegra Lawrence-Hardy

You can't hide it, nor do you want to

Assimilation only takes you so far. Race and gender are often obvious after all.

"I realized for many of these people, their exposure to women of color is limited, often limited to household staff. They have never met a person like me. If I was going to represent everyone [in the race], I had to do well and exceed expectations.

I have to give Judge Susan Black [United States Court of Appeals for the Eleventh Circuit] credit for helping me with this issue. I was worried about the fact that there were so few people of color at firms. I was wringing my hands. Judge Black told me, 'Wherever you go, there is a spotlight on you. You can use it for good or not. It's not your choice. You don't get to be anonymous.' "

—Allegra Lawrence-Hardy

"You don't have to leave who you are at the door. Absolutely not. You don't have to start playing golf, pretending like race doesn't matter. People want to be able to talk about it freely. You can't walk around with a chip on your shoulder. . . .

I just came back from a seminar on being a successful associate. I told the partner [who mentored me] the advice I gave to the associates: find an old white guy with a big book of business. He threw his head back, mouth

68

open, and laughed. It's OK to talk about race, joke about it. It's good for you to be who you are, recognize it doesn't have to be a source of tension."

—Sulee Clay

And why shouldn't you be proud of your race and gender?

"I'm a black woman. I'm very proud of it. I would not be at a place where I couldn't be myself. You can't ever pay me enough to do that."

—Tracy High

"I've always taken a perverse pleasure in putting my ethnicity out there and making people stop and think. Calling them 'gringos.' I'll make remarks and make people stop and think. I talk about Puerto Rico, how I grew up, how they grew up, rather than sit there with a chip on my shoulder. . . .

All of my artwork [in my office] tells about Puerto Rico. I go [to Puerto Rico] regularly; my family comes [to town] and I bring them here. I talk Spanish regularly with people here who speak it. And someone will say, 'That's not fair. What are you talking about?' And I'll say, 'We're talking about you.' "[laughs]

—Carmen Toledo

You'll notice that I didn't include any strategies in this chapter. I wouldn't presume to tell you how to make choices about your race and ethnicity. That's a purely personal decision. Granted, there can be political implications to the choices you make.

My best advice? Be aware of your environment. What do you see other women of color doing? It doesn't mean that you have to make the same choices that they do *but* it doesn't hurt to have full information prior to making your choice.

PART THREE:

Should I Stay or Should I Go?

CHAPTER 8

The Imposter Complex

"The way to develop self-confidence is to do the thing you fear and get a record of successful experiences behind you. Destiny is not a matter of chance, it is a matter of choice; it is not a thing to be waited for, it is a thing to be achieved."

—William Jennings Bryan

What is the "Imposter Complex?" It's an inferiority complex. A more vivid description that one partner offered is the Imposter Complex is that fear you have when you're a baby associate that at any moment a partner is going to throw open your door, point a finger at you, and pronounce you as a fraud.

It's a dreaded affliction that can strike whether you're at the top of your class at law school or you've just gotten a pat on the back for a well-done completed project and been handed a new assignment that you have no idea how to do. It is no respecter of race or creed. But it typically strikes women.

Angela Payne James told me a funny story that she heard while on a panel at a conference:

"A woman of color GC gave the example of if there was a job opening for someone to provide breastfeeding services and they went to a woman and said, 'Hey we want you to be a breast feeder,' her response would be, 'Well wait I've only done it one time. And I only have one kid. And I'm not really that good at it. It was a little awkward for me.' Whereas a man would be like, 'I'll do it! I can do it!'"

—Angela Payne James

73

Note: If after hearing this definition of the Imposter Complex, it's not something you can relate to, you can skip this chapter. This is not one of your challenges. On the other hand, maybe it makes sense for you to read on because as you begin to mentor others, you may need to have an understanding of this issue, as some of the women you counsel may suffer from this malady.

One partner (who shall definitely remain anonymous) shared her experience of the Imposter Complex. At her law school, the administration posts a list of graduates near the end of 3L year. As she was checking the list, she was <u>sure</u> that her name wouldn't be there. (Never mind the fact that she'd completed all of her course requirements and done pretty well in her classes; facts are irrelevant when you suffer from the Imposter Complex.)

When she couldn't find her name on the list, she said to herself miserably, "I knew it! I just knew it!" A friend standing next to her said, "Congratulations!" And she said, "Congratulations for what?" The friend said, "You graduated *cum laude!*" Sure enough. She wasn't on the regular graduate list; there was a separate list for honors graduates. Unbelievable.

How could these people, the crème de la crème, ever have these fears? Let's put it this way. I loved the reaction of the partners I interviewed when I asked them whether they experienced the dreaded Imposter Complex as they were coming up as associates. Most of them started giggling. That told me they knew exactly what I was talking about even before I explained the term because they had experienced this affliction themselves.

> *"We [Tandy and her fellow first year women colleagues] cried a <u>lot</u> the first year. We cried a lot. [laughs] It's not funny; it's really sad. We were huge, big bundles of insecurity. And some of us working for people who took every opportunity to exploit that and make us feel not only stupid but like bad people overall."*
>
> —Lovita Tandy

> *"This partner took issue with everything I did. He told me that I wasn't a good writer, that I didn't know how to do legal analysis. He got me a writing coach who said my writing was excellent but the partner would still find fault.*
>
> *Honestly, especially at first, I had grand feelings of inadequacy. I thought, 'Maybe he's right, maybe I can't do this, maybe I should be doing something else.'*
>
> —Anonymous Attorney

74

"I did have [the imposter complex] early on because I was seeking out key assignments, and I'd get them. I argued my first case in the U.S. District Court as a first year. It was an age discrimination class action. I was assigned a summary judgment motion on a very critical issue.

I was sure I was committing malpractice. That someone would say something—the judge, the client, somebody. Not the partner though, he'd put me in this situation. I was sure somebody was going to say, 'What the hell is going on?!'

I remember being surrounded by boxes at the office. I didn't understand what was the purpose of a summary judgment. I understood the issues. I just didn't understand the procedure. I was thinking, 'I am a fraud. I should not be doing this. I don't know what I'm doing.'

I called the partner. He was in his garden! I'm fighting back tears. I say, 'Maybe we could do a mock run-through.' He says, 'You'll be great! See you at the airport.' I hung up the phone and dissolved into tears. I said to myself, 'I'm totally screwed.' I called my husband. He said, 'It's going to be fine. Walk me through your argument.'

It was nuts.

I argued the motion and we won it! It was awesome. I'll never forget it!

—Nicole Pierre

"I never feel smart enough. . . . I expect every day for someone to say, 'You have no idea what you're doing.'

I attribute it to being a woman more than a person of color. I try to be conscious of saying 'I guess,' 'I think.' I have to edit my emails. Even when I know the answer, I'll say, 'It seems to me. . .'

—Anonymous Attorney

How do you handle your insecurities when you start? They can feel pretty overwhelming. Sure, you have a law degree and managed to pass the bar, but you feel like you don't know much more than that.

When I practiced, I had this sense that I was missing something because it seemed to me that my fellow first-year associates knew more than I did. They always acted like they knew what they were doing. Which didn't make sense, since we'd started at the same time! But I lacked the confidence that they had. (I should point out here that most of my practice group colleagues were white males; so they probably thought they would make good breast feeders too.)

You've got to get past this block however. Otherwise, it *is* going to impede your ability to do good work, to grow in your knowledge, and ultimately to advance.

So what *can* you do?

Strategy #1: Give yourself a pep talk

"I find that I am [not] dealing with that on a day-to-day basis anymore but sometimes someone might call and say, 'Hey we want you to be involved in this pitch or this case.' And you know I do have that immediate reaction where I want to say, 'Well I haven't done that yet. I have lots of experiencing doing "X" but I haven't done exactly that.'

Which of course is silly because how often are you going to do something that you've exactly done 10, 15 times? And rather than seeing that as an opportunity, I would see it as a stressful situation because I didn't have absolute comfort level and mastery over whatever I was being asked to do. And would sometimes shy away from those.

But typically I will force myself to do it anyway and kind of chin up and get on my 'Yes I can do this' and 'I can provide this service' or 'I can provide this skill.' Give yourself the pep talk. But sometimes I still have to do that.

Whereas I think for some people, that whole internal dialogue doesn't happen. It's just, 'Yep, OK I can do that.'

And so I don't have quite the thing I had before where you're waiting for someone to knock on the door and say, 'Oops' [referring to my illustration of the Imposter Complex at the beginning of the chapter] because after awhile I would have to give myself a pep talk and say, 'Well wait a minute you did do all of these things you know. If it was coincidence or good luck, that would have run out a long time ago.'"

—Anonymous Attorney

Learning Points from Strategy #1:

- **Remind yourself of what you've accomplished this far.** Yes, I know you're not a partner yet, so you can't go over the achievements that got you to that level like the partner above. But accomplishments aren't limited to partners, are they? Do you think you would have gotten this far if you weren't already capable? Recognize that the fact that the firm hired you is a vote of confidence that you can do the work, and do it well.

  So before the Imposter Complex strikes, make a list of accomplishments. Stick it in your desk drawer so when this malady strikes, you can pull out your list and go over it.

- **You don't have to wait for someone else to pat you on the back.** Talk yourself up—to yourself! You can do it in your head or you can do it aloud (preferably when no one else is around.) But do it. Treat yourself the way you'd treat anyone you care deeply about.

76

If a friend came to you questioning her capabilities and you already know that she's an accomplished person, you'd remind her of those accomplishments. You'd encourage and support her. Be that person for yourself!

- **Memorize the last statement in the quote from the partner above.** *"If it was coincidence or good luck, that would have run out a long time ago."* Yes, I know you're just at the beginning of your career or midway in but life didn't begin the day you started practice. It started when you were born. And I've heard some incredible stories about the challenges that people have had to hurdle before they ever set foot in their firm. The fact that you've made it this far is a testament to your ability. Coincidence or good luck would have run out a long time ago.

Strategy #2: Review your accomplishments on a regular basis

"I look at my resume. You have credentials. It's not affirmative action because the machine that scored your SAT and LSAT didn't know what your race is. And my bio—I love my bio."

—Bettina Yip

Learning Points from Strategy #2:

- **Keep your resume and bio up to date.** As an added bonus, if you decide to look for another job, you'll be ready! In fact, I'd take Yip's bio approach one step further. Make a note each and every time you complete a new project at work. If you receive compliments, be sure to keep track of those.
- **Celebrate!** I don't mean that you have to take yourself out for an expensive dinner every time you add something to your list (although that's perfectly fine), but you can honor your accomplishment in small, meaningful ways: buy yourself some flowers, jump up and down the way kids do when they're proud of themselves, get a hug from your favorite person, take your kids on a picnic, say a prayer of thanks and gratitude. Give yourself a pat on the back. It reinforces the message to yourself that you are moving forward. You'll be surprised how quickly that list builds. And without it, it's easy to forget you've done anything at work, especially in the early days.

  Then every time the Imposter Complex strikes, you can look at your list of accomplishments and remind yourself of the challenges you have tackled since you've been at the firm.

Strategy #3: Rely on your religious faith

"I believe that God has blessed me with many opportunities, so it's not about me. You aren't saying, 'It is me and I'm great. I'm super-smart and I can do anything on my own.' You really are saying, 'If God has blessed me with these opportunities, then God has provided me with [a way to succeed].' "

—Angela Payne James

Learning Points from Strategy #3:

- **Don't check your faith at your office door.** Bring it to work with you because it can sustain you.

  In Christianity, we are taught to have confidence because God is with us always. In fact: *"Christ lives in me."* (Galatians 2:19). That means that you are most certainly not doing this on your own; God is with you.

  Furthermore, if, as Payne James states above, God has blessed you with this opportunity and succeeding is what you desire in your heart, then God will provide you with the path. It doesn't mean that you won't have obstacles along the way of course. But we can overcome those obstacles with the Lord's help. *"If God is for us, who can be against us?"* (Romans 8:28)

  That old Imposter Complex isn't baggage we're meant to lug around. Remember: *"I can do all things through Christ who strengthens me."* (Philippians 4:13). Not some things, *all* things.

  Whatever your religious faith, allow it to empower you when your Imposter Complex tries to flare up.

What if someone is deliberately triggering your Imposter Complex?

Unfortunately, not everyone you work with at the firm is going to have your best interests at heart. In fact, you may find that there is the occasional person who seems to enjoy making your life miserable.

"When I started here, I felt terribly isolated because two of my colleagues, who were both minorities, one a woman of color, were extremely nasty. They didn't just shun me, they talked about me behind my back, told my boss I didn't know what I was doing, didn't share information.

So for at least six months I was depressed. But I lost ten pounds and I looked fantastic!"*

—Anonymous Attorney

*You've got to give this attorney credit for keeping her sense of humor.

Strategy #4: Get an outside opinion

Tandy describes a similar experience in Strategy #2, Chapter 6. The senior associate's behavior was so challenging that Tandy even considered leaving her firm. When I asked her what made her stay, she said:

> "Melba Hughes. [Melba Hughes is a legal recruiter in Atlanta, GA and also an African-American woman.] I didn't want to stick it out. By March of my first year I was in tears every, every day. I hated working for this guy. He was a pain in the behind.
>
> I went to see Melba. I said, 'Oh I hate it. I can't stand it. I've got to go.' And she was pretty much like, 'Look, I don't place first years.' And I said, 'Oh please, please, please, please, please.' And she was like, 'Well, I will help you.' And she did.
>
> But not how I intended. You know she set up interviews and I actually had another job. But through the process I was talking to her and I was explaining what went on. She just got really quiet and she was like, 'Do you want to be a lawyer?' I said, 'Yes, I've always wanted to be lawyer.' 'Do you want to be a good lawyer?' 'Yes.' And she's like, 'Well then you can't leave. Your self esteem is so low that you will not succeed anywhere. You've just got to, you've just got to stay. And we've got to fix it. You're too broken to be any good to anyone right now.'
>
> And I was. I thought I was the stupidest person on the face of God's green earth."

—Lovita Tandy

Learning Points from Strategy #4:

- **Find wise counsel.** Legal recruiters have seen and heard it all. So they have perspective. Find one you feel comfortable with and develop a relationship. You'll get a two-fold benefit: they can give you a reality-check, as well as keep you apprised of job opportunities just right for you.
- **Do what's best for you.** I'm going to offer a counter opinion. I had a similar experience to Tandy's but I took a different path. I left one of my jobs because I was working with a difficult person. (There were other factors motivating me to leave, but I'm pretty sure if I hadn't had to deal with that particular challenge, I probably would have stayed.) My mentors advised me to leave.

  But here's why: my experience was affecting my health, my outlook on life, and obviously, my confidence. Is it worth it to stay to prove that you can rise above adversity? I don't think there's an easy answer for that one. This, yet again, is where the value of having mentors is so glaringly obvious.

79

May you never have to go through such a nightmare. But let's be prepared, just in case.

Strategy #5: Get an inside advantage

"Having other friends in the practice group made a difference. Having Scott and Shelly Blews [Tandy's mentors] made a difference, you know, because Scott was the same year as this other person [the bully] and having Scott there to say, 'No, [your work] is actually above average for what we would expect of a first year.' Being able to sanity-check it.

And I think you know beforehand I was sanity-checking it with the other women, the other first years but they don't really know either. 'Cause we all started together. And so being able to sanity-check it with Scott. And being able to trust him enough to do that."

—Lovita Tandy

Learning Points from Strategy #5:

* **Now do you understand why I say you won't survive without mentors?** You've got to have someone with whom you've built a relationship with enough trust so that you can go to them when times get rough. You've got to have someone who can help you "sanity-check" it, as Tandy describes above. Your judgment is likely going to be a bit impaired in your first few years.

    I have a theory about this one. Law school is about taking bright, capable people and breaking them down. Breaking them down to build them up. Into people who can think like lawyers. Now I'm sure not all law schools are like that, but I've heard enough horror stories about the twisting of the Socratic method into a form of torture (and experienced one of my own) to back up my theory.

    As a result, when you graduate, you've been rebuilt into someone who can think like a lawyer, yes, but your self esteem has also taken a severe beating. Some recover quickly. Heck, some are never affected. (You know those people from law school who could be told to their faces "You're an idiot" and it would have absolutely no impact on them.) But lots have been, well, traumatized.

    So just when you're expected to come in and be this dynamic superstar, instead you show up as a quivering mass of Jell-O.

    That's why it's so important to connect with more senior associates and partners who offer a helping hand. They know what you've been through, but more importantly they've come out of it and now have a clear perspective of the situation.

- **Girlfriends are good, yes, but you also need more senior people.** As you can see from Tandy's story, she was trying to do a "sanity-check" with her fellow first years, but they didn't know any more than she did. You need someone on a higher level to assess the situation.

Strategy #6: Hang in there

Remember the Anonymous Attorney in Chapter 8 who was suffering because two of her colleagues, both minorities, were shunning her and talking about her behind her back? I asked her how in the world she survived that:

"After six months, my company hired a good friend. So I started feeling more at ease. And my boss recognized how they were treating me and told me that he supported me.

At this point [six years later], one [of the bad guys] has left and the other I don't have to deal with anymore. Plus I've got two additional people I'm close to here. So the tables have turned a little."

—Anonymous Attorney

Learning Points from Strategy #6:

- **This too shall pass.** I wish that I could offer something that could magically wipe these occurrences out. But there is no such magic wand. As you can see though, persistence and waiting it out do work. In the words of a song sung by Oleta Adams, "Everything must change. Nothing stays the same."
- Remember the difficult experience I described at my job in Strategy #4 above? A year after I left, my nemesis was let go and my good friend, who was at the same level as I, took her place. If I'd stayed, that means I probably would have been promoted to the role my nemesis had! Would it have been worth it to stick around then? Again, that's a very personal decision I trust you to make. But know that if you choose to stay, things will change.

    And just in case I haven't hammered on this point enough, if you do good work, you'll develop influential supporters, like Anonymous Attorney's boss above.

Not everyone has this dreaded affliction

I was sure that every lawyer I interviewed would have some variation of the Imposter Complex, whether large or small. I was wrong. With hindsight I think, how naïve. Or maybe stereotypical. Of course, not everyone carries around an inferiority complex. We can learn from these women too!

Here's Allegra Lawrence-Hardy's explanation:

"I've never had [the Imposter Complex.] When I saw that question, I laughed because people often ask. Does that make me cocky or narcissistic? [laughing]

We're not rocket scientists, brain surgeons. Lots of people can be very good at it.

It helped having gone to a well-regarded law school. Nobody intimidates you."

—Allegra Lawrence-Hardy

Clay agrees:

"I got over that at Harvard undergrad. In law school [also Harvard], I thought, 'Those guys aren't that smart.'

Going to Harvard [undergrad] you learn you can hang. That gives you confidence.

You're not going to know the answer to every question. You go to law school to learn how to find the answers. There are 3,000 people at this firm. Someone knows the answer.

I did wonder when I was going to start feeling like a lawyer. It takes about four to five years.

Understand your role. Your role is not to be an encyclopedia."

—Sulee Clay

CHAPTER 9

Is It Our Responsibility to Uphold the Race?

"From what we get, we can make a living; what we give, however, makes a life."

—Arthur Ashe

Let me state the obvious: The incredible opportunities described in these pages haven't always been available to women of color. In fact, if you read Part One (you did read Part One, right? Remember you were supposed to? OK, enough nagging), you saw that we have only had these opportunities pretty recently.

Let me state another obvious fact: There aren't that many of us at the Big Firms. So those of us who are there often feel as if we have a responsibility. We are representing our race.

Note: This chapter is less about strategies and more a discussion of this concept of responsibility. Because it's such a personal issue, I don't think it's appropriate to offer advice. I've included this chapter in the book, however, because it definitely shapes and informs a woman of color's experience at the firm.

*"I feel like I have a responsibility to represent my race well. **What that means is up to interpretation.** I don't want to propagate stereotypes of Asian-Americans, that we're submissive, only good at math and science.*

I want to inspire us to go into law because it's not dominated by Asian-Americans. Our parents still want their kids to be doctors or engineers.

It's exponentially more difficult for an Asian-American to make partner at a law firm than other races. *If there are more Asian-American in-house counsel, they may see Asian-Americans in firms as rainmakers because networking is a major activity in the Asian-American community."*

—Bettina Yip

"I was always taught, 'Do unto others as you would like for them to do unto you.' That goes broadly, not just race. People struggled to sacrifice for you to be where you are. With that comes a responsibility to help other people.

We all have a responsibility regardless of race. I feel I'm particularly situated to help other people of color, women, and women of color because people did that for me."

—Angela Payne James

"When and where I enter, the whole race enters with me. In most circles I'm the only black female there. Whether I'm sitting across the table from Jimmy Hoffa negotiating contracts or in a Senate office.

It carries a big—it's a big responsibility. I think about it a lot."

—Nicole Pierre

"Associates of color are not succeeding well at my firm as they should. I've been talking to other partners. What can we do? How can we get down to basics? It's important that partners of color and senior associates of color pass on and share that information with young associates of color. Their success is important."

—Anonymous Attorney

"I think it's very important to have women and women of color visible in a partnership. Ideally in the management of the firm.

It's being willing to step up and take on leadership roles. I know what sacrifices that means because of time. It's very difficult.

Everyone can do it in different ways. Mentoring, going to firm management and saying, 'Put me in a role that's more visible.' Getting on committees at the firm.

If that doesn't happen, the women's perspective and the diverse perspective is never going to be there."

—Lisa Kobialka

"My view is that there are many who have gone before me personally, professionally and in our race who have made sacrifices.

Like when I was in [grade school] I wrote a paper about the first black woman millionaire, Madame C.J. Walker. That was really fascinating that at that time, given those conditions, that someone was able to create a business when the odds said that's not possible.

It's stories like that that have always inspired me. . . .

I feel responsible to guide and give direction. I've always been interesting in doing that. To the extent someone is interesting in learning to excel, I give input.

I think it's the right thing to do. To help someone else. It's not limited to African-Americans or minorities but I do have a special passion for my race and my heritage."

—Charmaine Slack

"I want to use my education and experience to do work on behalf of [Native American] tribes. For the longest time, no one knew the system and had a vested interest in the best outcome for the community. It was the primary reason I decided to go to law school.

I feel a responsibility to use it to give back to my community, to help tribes grow and prosper, maintain tribal sovereignty."

—Danelle Smith

That begs the question. *Is* it our responsibility to uphold the race? And if so, just how far does that responsibility extend?

The question brings to mind the recent history of the Citadel, the military college of Charleston, SC. If you're not familiar with this drama, the Citadel went coed after a long and contentious court battle. The very first woman, Shannon Faulkner, was admitted as a student and then left shortly thereafter because she decided that she didn't want the opportunity.

There were very strong feelings on both sides of this issue and it made for a very tense environment on campus. I was privy to a lot of what was going on because I was part of a team brought in to provide leadership and sexual harassment training for the cadets shortly afterwards.

It was fascinating to hear the cadets talk about Faulkner's experience, especially the women cadets. (While Faulkner was the first, she certainly wasn't the last. Several other women admitted to the college shortly after her said that they were determined to prove that they were worthy of the honor and would graduate.) On the one hand, if she didn't want to be there, they definitely didn't want her there. On the other hand, the fact that she dropped out was regarded by some of the male cadets as a clear indication that women couldn't hack it. Some of the female cadets felt that whether she wanted to or not, she should have stayed and completed her education, as her leaving had greater significance than that she personally couldn't handle it. They felt that it reflected poorly on *all* women interested in attending a military college.

When there are very few of you in an environment, unfortunately, you are living in a fishbowl. What you do and don't do is often not just a reflection upon you but also your kind, whether it be gender or ethnicity or both. It may not be fair, it may not be right, but it is what it is.

There is also an often unintended impact on those like you. They are watching you closely too. And if you decide to leave, they may wonder, "If she didn't make it, what chance do I have?"

> *"I feel a huge responsibility to our race. I think that it impacts me every day. I feel like it has kept me going when I've wanted to stop. I don't see it as the Imposter Complex but there's always this part where you feel like you have to prove.*
>
> *And if you're the only one, you're the only one available to prove or disprove the theory. And there's a fear of, if you leave, then 'Ah ha, there you go. Told you those people can't cut it. They're not made for this.'*
>
> *And if you stumble or fall you will be looked at, not like a white male who stumbles or falls, but looked at as conclusive proof that everyone who is behind you who looks like you therefore will stumble and fall.*
>
> *And you feel it from everywhere. It's—that's not something that you feel just from, you know, like the white males above you. You feel that from the minorities below you.*
>
> *I mean, I remember when I got pregnant, other minorities in the firm saying, 'How could you do this? You are so close to partner. How could you do this to us?' And I was like, 'Well, your parents really should have had that discussion with you BUT let me break it down. When a man and a woman love each other. . . .' [laughs]*
>
> *But it's a lot of pressure and I think that I can't even honestly tell you whether I would still be here today if it weren't for the women and minorities behind me. But if I had to guess, I'd say 'No.' I don't need this much money. I don't need this much stress.*
>
> *There are people here I've worked with for a long time of whom I'm very fond. I know where they live. I can see them on the weekends."*
>
> —Lovita Tandy

I then said to Tandy, "So essentially you're taking one for the team."

86

She agreed, saying: *"If I leave, they'll feel like they can't make it."*

—Lovita Tandy

Here's a different perspective:

"I definitely feel a responsibility to the race. First of all, to be a good mentor to those children who want to be lawyers or finish high school, go to college. I do feel like the whole idea of the Talented Tenth [has merit]. I have a responsibility to pull the other 90% along behind.

I don't know that that feeling of responsibility has affected my career choice. It definitely affects what I do with my position, whatever I'm doing, to help other people."

—J. Shontavia Jackson

And another:

"I feel a great deal of responsibility to my race. It's vitally important that we make it in Corporate America. If we're not here, you can't be a participant.

The hard part of that also means staying when it's hard. If we don't stay and do it, we have a tough argument complaining that we aren't in the corridors of Corporate America."

—Tracy High

Here's an interesting (and somewhat funny) perspective:

"I made the decision to marry an Asian-American man. There are so many 'out marriages' [Asian-American women marrying Caucasian men]. There's huge anecdotal evidence supporting this, huge. I feel like the message 'out marriages' send is that Asian-American men are not good enough, white men are a step up. If I became successful, I didn't want anyone to think I had to marry a white man to be successful. Now that's not the only reason I married him. [laughs]"

—Bettina Yip

What my responsibility is to my race was a question I considered very carefully before leaving the practice of law. I came to the following conclusions:

Yes, I do have a responsibility to my race. Because my ancestors felt an obligation to me, I have been provided with opportunities that I would not otherwise have. Without the sacrifices of my ancestors, African-American people would not be where we are today.

But just what that responsibility entails is not so cut and dried. Surely, it is not my responsibility to stay in the practice of law if I do not want to be here. In fact, by choosing to do so, I may be missing out on other opportunities by which I can represent my race more fully and more joyfully. Wouldn't that be a shame?

Am I grateful that I have been given the opportunity to work in the legal field? Yes, I am. What I decided did not make sense though is for me to take that gratitude and use it as a hammer on myself. Saying things like, "I am being ungrateful then to be unhappy and to want to leave the law."

Here's what else we have to be grateful for: Yes, our ancestors were fighting for us to have these specific opportunities. <u>But</u> they were also fighting for us to have the opportunity to make choices, that we can choose work that's fulfilling. That if we want to leave the law to pursue work that's meaningful to us, we live in a time and country ("life, liberty, and the pursuit of happiness," remember) where we can do that.

So, I decided that, of course, I was grateful for my legal job. But I knew that if I chose to do something else with my J.D., something that engaged me, I'd feel even more grateful.

I believe that this choice is a very personal one. As you can see, there are differing perspectives on this issue. That's OK. That difference of opinion just illustrates that there are no simple black and white answers to the question, only shades of gray.

Wouldn't it be nice though just to be able to exist without the boundaries of race? To be able to just be? Or not?

"My hope is that you don't think about my race first, my gender first.
But then someone said to me 'I don't see you as black.' A colleague said
that. That made me really angry. I really, really struggled with that."

—Nicole Pierre

"Funny, isn't it," I said to Pierre. On the one hand, we don't want always to be seen as "That nice black attorney." On the other hand, when someone tells us that they "don't see us as black," we see that not as a compliment but as an insult. The implication somehow is that the black race is the opposite of what we are. If we are competent, speak well, write well, socialize well, then we are not "like the rest of" our race. What we want is to be judged by is our capabilities, not our race; <u>but</u> for racial stereotypes not to exist. A tall order but that's what we want. Pierre agreed.

88

"I'm not trying to be black. I am just trying to be competent. I want to be thought of as an outstanding lawyer, litigator, lobbyist or mother."

—Nicole Pierre

A lot of the lawyers I spoke to felt a responsibility to children, both their own and others.

"I want to impart to my children that they have every right to be there, as much as anyone else. I hope that they're not going to see race but capability.

It shouldn't matter that I'm black. But every day that's what people see. I wish that wasn't the case. Why not, 'She's a smart girl.'

—Simone Boayue-Gumbs

"I feel a responsibility to make sure our children understand the importance of putting their best foot forward. Doing things that you may not want to do, but you deserve to be there. I've never felt like I shouldn't be somewhere. Why shouldn't I be here? You deserve a seat at the table. I want my children to really understand that."

—Nicole Pierre

"With young people I think it's important to feel like I can help to raise the expectations we have [on the reservation]. I don't think they're high enough. If you drop out of high school, don't go to college, get pregnant as a teenager, there is no social stigma [in my community]. It's not a given you're going to college. If you don't, families say that's OK. It's OK for some. But we should not settle for that always."

—Danelle Smith

Now some would argue that this country has gotten past its racial biases. Look at the fact that we can and do thrive in large law firms and other industries. Look at the fact that we are represented at top universities. Heck, Monica, look at the fact that this country put the Obama family in the White House and Sonia Sotomayor has been appointed a Justice of the Supreme Court!

Yes, these accomplishments are a testament to how far we've come. Absolutely. But as Nicole Pierre said to me in our interview, *"Regardless of having an African-American president, we still have a long way to go. In D.C. we see it as glaring."*

The struggles aren't behind us just yet. I hope you realize that that is so by the very existence of this book.

CHAPTER 10

On Becoming a Golden Child

"Too much of a good thing can be wonderful."

—Mae West

What is a "Golden Child?" I first heard this term during a summer clerkship. A Golden Child is a summer associate or associate about whom expectations are exceedingly high. This person is eagerly anticipated by the firm and if there are any perks to be had, such as good projects, early hands-on experience, working one-on-one with partners, this individual will be granted them.

How do you get the Golden Child label? I think Angela Payne James describes it best in Chapter Three. It all begins even before your first year at the firm. The initial labeling can occur as early as your very first interviews. When you interviewed with a firm during a screening interview at law school, then when you're invited to the firm for a callback, the firm is paying close attention.

Surprising in a way, isn't it? You haven't even done any work yet! And, yet, it proves a point I'm sure you've heard many times before in your life: first impressions matter. Dearly.

So how do you impress the firm and acquire Golden Child status?

What I'm about to say shouldn't surprise you: It doesn't hurt if you attend a top law school. Please don't shoot the messenger. And if you're already in law school, obviously, this isn't a comment for you. It's for the pre-law students and those contemplating a second career reading the book. Select your law school carefully. Get into the best school you possibly can. Or at the very least, select a school that provides the education and programs that you desire, as well a placement program that will get you where you want to go. (If you're already in law school, work with what you've got—get excellent grades, fight for top ranking, develop relationships with influential professors who can give good recommendations for you, polish your interview skills.)

But there's also a LOT to be said for how you present yourself in the interviews. Do you come across as poised and confident? Interesting and thoughtful? Witty and charming?

(You'll notice I said, "come across as." That means, while you may be quaking on the inside, if you can project a sense of calm and positive on the exterior, that's half the battle.)

I remember callbacks as being marathon days. It's interview after interview, not to mention lunch and dinner. You don't want to let things slip at meals either. How you handle ordering, eating, and answering questions tells the firm a lot about you. They're watching.

And, yes, they're watching again all throughout the summer. How are you handling your assignments, the work load? Are you getting assignments done on time? Is your work product excellent? Are you an "eager beaver?" Do you "fit" the firm culture? (That one is easier said than explained. Fit is an elusive quality; one that I'm sure a lot of firms would say, "I know it when I see it." The point is not that you have to be like everyone around you. After all, diversity is a quality that's often prized by firms. What's more important is whether people *like* you. Yep, it boils down to like. Whether they feel like they can identify with you, work with you, spend late nights at the office with you, get through reams of documents with you.)

And as if that's not enough, what about the onslaught of firm social events? Do you handle summer associate events well? Are you attending, participating, mingling? What a smorgasbord of opportunities to cement your reputation as a star! (Remember, I never said this journey would be easy.) As is the converse: there are plenty of opportunities to tarnish your reputation—are you the person everyone remembers falling into the pool and needing to be rescued from drowning because you were rip-roaring drunk or perhaps you were found sprawled out asleep on the floor in the firm library?

That would never be you, you say. I believe it. If there is one thing that ambitious women of color understand is that, like it or not, we are often held to a higher standard. We have to comport ourselves with the utmost decorum, work harder and longer, and do better work than the majority race. It may not be fair, but it is better to acknowledge that reality and make choices from there than it is to pretend it isn't true.

It is also important to recognize that you can't rest on your laurels. Yes, if you begin with the reputation of being a Golden Child, it can cushion the blow for those early days when you make a few mistakes (because I say again, you *will* make a few mistakes). But you cannot rely on keeping the label just because it was granted to you as a summer associate.

You have to work at maintaining your Golden Child status until you reach your bright and shining goal, making partner. And guess what? Even then the game is not over. Once you make partner, you're starting at level one again in a sense; after all, you're a baby partner. You have to continue working at your Golden Child status if you want to make equity partner and, yes, believe it or not, *maintain* equity partner status. (But that's a story for another day and another book.)

Let's look at some strategies for maintaining Golden Child status throughout your associate career. But first. . . .

If you don't come in as a "Golden Child" from the very beginning, are you doomed?

"I think people get labeled pretty quickly in law firms and it does become a bit of a self-fulfilling prophecy. I think I did not come in the door as one. Some people come in the door as one from the summer program. That decision has already been made at many, many firms. And now—I think I can explain it better now as a partner than I could have articulated what happened when I was an associate. **But what happened is I did the most fabulous job I knew how to do for those first few projects that I had for Lane Dennard [Tandy's mentor], only one of which was billable.** *The others had to do with a paper and a book that he was writing.* <u>Busted my tail</u>.

And then word of mouth. [T]here's a partner's meeting and people going around the table saying, 'How is so-and-so, how are people doing?' And Lane is like, I'm sure what happened is he was like, 'Oh you know I'm giving all these first years you know these non-billable assignments and Lovita's are getting to me on time and they're better than everybody else's.' Well then natural selection and natural instincts kick in. 'Then I want to use her. I want to use her too.' **It's word of mouth.**"

—Lovita Tandy

"I definitely was not one of those [golden children]. The way I look at it— my job was to make the partner's life easy. I look at what it is they really

want with the project. It's different from partner to partner. Then I became invaluable to them. Time and time they come back because it was easy."

—Lisa Kobialka

Strategy #1: Be willing to put in the time

"Frankly . . . a lot of women don't stay because the job requires you 24/7. It requires a lot of time. A lot of people exit for that very reason. They take a job that's easier on family commitments. It's tough for women.

It's an investment of time. Being available to people. Making people feel you're always there, putting your best foot forward. [The firm knows it] can rely on you to service the client in a way that's profitable and consistent. You have to be servicing the clients well or even better.

In that way, this environment doesn't see color. If you're providing good work and working your butt off, they don't care if you're black, yellow, or green. They could care less."

—Simone Boayue-Gumbs

Learning Points from Strategy #1:

- **It's going to take time.** We live in an instant gratification society. It's not your fault. It's just that our culture, technology, among other things, has sped everything up; so if you're not an "overnight success," it's easy to feel discouraged. Making partner is, just as Boayue-Gumbs described it, an investment of your time. Recognize that up front and you'll be better off. You can focus on doing quality work, building excellent relationships, developing your legal expertise and know-how—instead of fretting over the next seven to ten years about not being an overnight success.

Strategy #2: View the partners and senior associates as your clients

"Clients aren't just external clients. There are also internal clients—the partners and associates you do work for. So when they approach, giving you assignments, view them as clients. That perspective helps you to frame how you respond. When you give a project that type of focus, you are viewed as someone who is client-focused."

—Charmaine Slack

Learning Points from Strategy #2:

- **Everyone is a client.** This approach is how in-house counsel views the departments in their company. You should take advantage of

94

this strategy at the Big Firm as well because it's guaranteed to help you accelerate your career.

Strategy #3: Ask for what you want

"When I was a fourth or fifth year I was put on a case that ended up being very significant for the firm. I had previously gone to my practice group leader to request more nuts and bolts litigation experience and had specifically asked to get put on a case that was going to trial.

As it turned out, a partner who was not in my practice group but who sat on the same floor [Mike Kenny] had such a case. He knew me and had seen me working hard. When the associate working with him on the case left the firm, I was put on the case. It went to trial, and we ended up getting the largest verdict in the firm's history at the time and one of the top ten plaintiff's verdicts that year. Because it was a contingency fee case, which was not common for us at the time, the firm made a significant profit. That case—and the support of my practice group leader and the lead trial partner—really helped me increase my profile at the firm and gain invaluable trial experience."

—Angela Payne James

"Cubans say (I'm Puerto Rican but this is a Cuban saying) that 'the one who doesn't cry doesn't suck.' If you don't cry, you don't get the bottle. If you're happy just sitting there [doing your work], management has no incentive to change your status."

—Carmen Toledo

Learning Points from Strategy #3:

- **Speak up.** The Cuban saying Toledo mentions is apropos, whether we're talking about asking for the assignments you want to asking what skills sets you need to add to your arsenal to be a strong candidate for partner to speaking up for yourself when you think it's time to be made partner.
- **Be strategic.** Yes, you should take on assignments that are offered. *And* you should consider what kind of work you want to have to build your career. Then pursue that kind of work.
- **Be brave.** As you can see from Payne James' story, practice group leaders don't bite. You can state your case in such a way that is both polite and persistent.
- **You should be sick of this one by now. <u>Do good work</u>.** You don't know who is watching. The case, the project that makes your career might not even be one within your practice group. Mike

95

Kenny wasn't in Payne James' practice group. He was on her floor. Make it your job to impress the heck out of anyone you come in contact with. You'll be rewarded.

Strategy #4: Adapt

"You really have to have a thick skin.

It is a different environment. Not because it's a white male environment but because it is a business environment. Everybody has to adapt to it."

—Tracy High

Learning Points from Strategy #4:

- **Put your armor on.** Develop that thicker skin. Remember that you're in a business environment. That's a tough environment, period. The stronger you become, the more you'll thrive.

Strategy #5: Own up to your mistakes

What could making mistakes possibly have to do with being a Golden Child, you ask. I said it before, I'll say it again: you're going to make mistakes. What separates you from the pack is how you handle them.

"Own up to it. Say, 'This is how I'll fix it.' Guys are good at getting defensive. They say, 'The junior associate screwed up.' 'My secretary did it.' 'You told me this.' They hide it. Those are bad moves.

Good will is huge. Obviously you want to minimize mistakes. But they will happen. Own up to them.

I've had to call clients and say I screwed up. People respect you more. For the most part, clients don't care, as long as they're getting the service they want."

—Sulee Clay

Learning Points from Strategy #5:

- **Admit you made a mistake.** This is not the time to resort to the childish strategy of finding someone else to blame. If it truly is your fault, own up to it. It can be hard to do, but it's also the right thing to do. It shows you have integrity.
- **Come up with a solution and present that when you share your mistake.** No one likes to be presented with problems. If you can come in with the problem and the solution, it shows you have initiative. Even if your superior decides to go with another strategy,

you've demonstrated your ability to problem-solve, as well as work under pressure.

- **Don't blame others; it's so cowardly.** Not only might this damage your relationship with your superiors, but also it certainly won't endear you to your fellow associates, the paralegals, and the secretaries if you point the finger at them. Remember, you have to work with these people going forward, and they're often some of your best resources at the firm. And it certainly won't endear you to your superior if you blame them either. There's a move that could really backfire.

Strategy #6: Want it . . . more than anything else

I asked Tandy to tell me what she thinks separates her from her women of color peers who don't make it to this level of success.

> *"I think they don't have any way to sanity-check what is going on around them. And in the absence of that you're very likely to internalize things and feel like you are the problem. That's just the woman's way to do things.*
>
> *I think there are a lot of people who just don't want it. There are a lot of people who go to law school and don't want to be lawyers. There are a lot of people who go to law school and don't want to be lawyers in a Big Firm. It's hard. **It is really, really hard and you've really, really got to want it a lot.** And not everyone does, of any race or gender.*
>
> *I think the emotional toil that it takes on us is so different than the emotional toil it takes on the average white male. You're dealing with cultural issues, trying to fight stereotypes, trying to find your feet as a lawyer. All of these things in addition to what the average white male is going through. You know, I mean, you're trying to find the confidence to disagree with a 60-year-old white man, which is an experience that most of us have never had. I mean, even if you're a female associate, you know, maybe your uncle's a 60-year-old white man. I mean you have sat there and had a conversation with a 60-year-old white man at some point in your life. I never have.*
>
> ***You kind of have to want it almost to the exclusion of everything else.** And very few people do."*

—Lovita Tandy

I asked Tandy, "What do you mean when you say 'to the exclusion of everything else?' What's 'everything else?'"

" 'Everything else' is—I went to college with you, I may see you once a year.

I'm a natural introvert . . . I am physically exhausted and when I am not working, I am not going out to dinner, I've got to just 'veg.' Can't do it. Physically cannot do it."

—Lovita Tandy

Strategy #7: Love it . . . or learn to love it

"I really like my job. That makes a huge difference. [It's very rare that I] don't want to come to work on Monday.

Actual contentment with the job makes it much easier to be successful. Because I was cheerful."

—Elizabeth Reza

"For associates coming up looking for a job, the right fit, you need to be flexible. [Let's say] you really want to be a corporate lawyer but there are not as many opportunities. But you have an opportunity to be a litigator. Do it and embrace it. Everything you learn will help you. You'll be surprised.

[Let's say] you want to work in the city. But the opportunity is outside. Understand your priorities. If you're going to be miserable, don't do it.

You've got to love what you do. If you don't, don't do it. It's too stressful. Make sure you're passionate about it."

—Lisa Kobialka

Learning Points from Strategy #7:

- **Yes, you can find passion here.** Law is such a demanding profession but as you can see from the partners above, you can like it, love it, even feel passionate about it. Be clear about what it is you want from the law and go after that because that's where the day-to-day enjoyment, yes, even the passion, can be found.
- **Be flexible.** And then on the other hand, you may not always be able to get what you want. I remember people being devastated because they didn't get into the practice group they wanted. That's when you really have to look at your priorities. Maybe it wasn't necessarily about that practice group but the kinds of experiences and opportunities you'd get there. Dig deep and figure out what's important to you. You might be surprised to find that you can get

what you want where you are. Or at best, be open-minded. As Kobialka says, you can learn wherever you are. In fact, you might be surprised.

Strategy #8: Set high expectations for yourself

When I asked Danelle Smith what set her apart from her peers who don't make it to this level of success, she laughed and said:

"That's the million dollar question . . . I don't know the answer to that. School came easy for me. That was a big factor. I liked school. I was curious, always wanted to learn, even still. I don't think I'll ever stop feeling like that. It's an internal drive. . . .

My environment was set up for me to do nothing and that would have been totally acceptable."

—Danelle Smith

Learning Points from Strategy #8:

- **You decide what your goals are.** Not all of us, heck, probably not most of us, were born with a silver spoon in our mouths. Some of us have made it this far only by the grace of God. We were surrounded by people with little or no expectations for their own lives and ours. That's why it's so important that you set your own expectations of what you can accomplish. Don't let your family, friends, peers, even the firm decide what your goals are. You decide how far, how high you're going to go. And don't let anyone pull you down or stop you or tell you that you're dreaming.

What about work/life balance?

Ah, work/life balance. Let me make a bit of a controversial statement here. I almost feel like whoever came up with this phrase should be shot.

Why? Because it implies that there is this perfect state in which work and life are balanced. I don't believe that's possible.

What I do believe is that work/life balance exists on a spectrum. While we can't achieve balance, we *are* in a state of perpetual motion, either moving towards balance or away from it. The question then become, which direction are you going in and how can you course-correct if you're heading away from balance?

I would also venture to say that at any given point, different areas of your life require more attention. For example, if you're tied up with

99

traveling for depositions, that's what gets your time. If you're planning your wedding or you have a child who, God forbid, is ill, those things get the bulk of your attention. So it's less about balancing in all areas at all times but balancing out overall over time.

Danelle Smith agrees:

> *"I think you're right. It's a constant struggle to [balance]. At any given point I wouldn't have ever been able to say that everything's balanced.*
>
> *I live by my calendar and to-do lists, both personally and professionally. I'm constantly evaluating what my priorities are and assessing whether they're in the right order."*

—Danelle Smith

I think Charmaine Slack describes balance beautifully:

> *"I recognize that to be functional, healthy—physically, mentally, emotionally, some level of balance is necessary. So if you're only working to the detriment of everything else, it's unlikely that you're truly content with work and life.*
>
> *If you don't have career satisfaction and you have family or other outside activities, then you're not fully content.*
>
> *You need some of both and anything in excess could border on faults."*

—Charmaine Slack

That's the philosophical side of the issue. Let's look at the practical side. Here's the study *Visible Invisibility*'s take on this issue:

> *"Unlike white men, most [women of color] did not have someone at home who could take care of household and child-rearing responsibilities. Most women, regardless of color, were primary breadwinners in their households; their incomes supported their families, so work/family conflicts were professionally and financially wrenching."*[1]

When I asked some of the women how they manage it all, here's what they had to say:

> *"I don't manage it all. My husband and I discussed in detail what we wanted for our family and how best to make sure that our children came first without relinquishing the careers we worked hard to build. We are on the same page in that regard and it makes a big difference in our abil-*

---

[1] Visible Invisibility, p. 34

ity to support two careers. During the 4.5 years that I've had children, I've relied a lot on family, friends and trustworthy care givers to help support the family while my husband and I worked and sometimes traveled. It was difficult to admit that I couldn't do it all and that certain decisions and tasks could be outsourced so that I could continue to pursue my career. I was lucky that my parents and my in-laws lived in close proximity and could help us with childcare. At some point, we decided that hiring a nanny made sense for our family and we located a trustworthy person by word of mouth. We don't have a perfect system, but it works pretty well. I still feel guilty sometimes for not being a stay-at-home mom, but that's just not who I am.

I also made career changes when it made sense for me. I moved from firm life to in-house because I wanted a better balance. Luckily, I found it. When it was time to look for a new in-house position, it was a little easier to make the move because I had survived the big move from the firm to the corporate world just fine."

—Nicole Pierre

Here's another perspective:

"For women and women [of color], you've got to look for opportunities and when it's right for you. There's nothing worse than seeing an opportunity and you just had a baby. Work/life balance is a real challenge. It's a really tough one.

This is how I've been able to come to terms with it. It's learning to be able to let go and letting other people help out, both at work and at home. I've become a lot more flexible. There are times I have to sacrifice because that's what work demands and that's important. There are times I have to sacrifice because home life demands it. That is where you find balance."

—Lisa Kobialka

And another one:

"It's really hard. It's hard to have it all. It's hard to have it all early [in your career].

It's important to have a supportive partner because it's hard to do a full-time job and carry all of the home stuff well. [Reza is married with four children.]

I have to be comfortable with my decision. How much is going to be enough? I heard someone on a panel say, 'Look for someone [at work] who has a life you can imagine living. I can't imagine seeing my kids only in the morning and not at night and weekends.

101

One [of my mentors] gets in the office in the early morning. He's on his computer from 5—7 a.m. Then there's a gap. He does some stuff with his kids. I do that too—I eat breakfast with my kids and walk them to school. I try to achieve a set time at night [to leave the office]. [My mentor] leaves at 7:10 p.m. every night.

Others might say, 'No way.' That is not the life I want to have.

I chose this practice area for lifestyle reasons.

We [Reza and her husband] do a menu for the week and we go grocery shopping. I knew an associate who said she cooked a huge batch of something and she and her family ate it all week. I thought, 'What?!' But if you're OK with it and your kids are OK with it, that's what matters."

—Elizabeth Reza

And another one:

"It would be nice if I had a driver and a wife [laughs] but since I don't. . . .

I came here as a lateral, a fourth year. Three or four years later I took an Of Counsel position. I was full-time but without the expectations of business development or the kind of high billable hours you would have to put in as a partner. I did that for seven or eight years, maybe more. I had a second child while I was Counsel. When I had the second child, I had a nanny who lived in our house. . . . That helped. The children were fed when I got home. I only had to worry about the weekends. If I had to work, I would bring them in with a little DVD player.

Once the girls were in school, I put my name in for partner and made partner.

It's just day to day. Every day is an adventure. I have a very supportive husband. He's a consultant so he has a flexible schedule. He takes care of them in the afternoon. When I get home, he'll go back to work.

In a way technology helps . . . I can go home at 6, 6:30, have dinner with them. I can do some more work or usually I get up really early and do more work.

It's not really a question of balance. It's a tightrope. [laughs]

I'm not meant to be a stay-at-home mom. I would not be doing my children any favors by staying at home. I like working."

—Carmen Toledo

Here's a situation some might kill for:

"The key to what I do is my mother and father, Geraldine and John Adams. I'm in a unique situation because my mother takes full-time care of my children. She is the balance. She provides the balance in my life.

I made a conscious decision to work in an industry located either 3,000 miles to the West in California or 60 miles North in New York. But yet I chose to live in Princeton, NJ. To live somewhere I know I could provide a nearly ideal environment for my children. My parents also live in Princeton. It's a multigenerational environment for my children.

It's a trade-off. I trade off time with friends. I trade off a couple of hours with my children. I needed to make sure my kids were great. I felt more comfortable with my mom as a caretaker. I wanted to continue to work.

What I tell people is, you can have it all but you can't have it all at once. Prior to having children, my husband and I lived the cool New York life. We gave up a lot of it so that our children could be in an ideal situation.

I don't like my commute. People ask me all the time, 'How do you do it?" It's one and a half hours one way. You know how I do it? It's easy. I sit on a train and I read a book. Never for a moment am I worried about my kids. I am able to concentrate at work. No rushing home because the nanny has to leave. Sure I want to be the first person there when my kids skin their knees. But given that I'm a working mom, kids don't skin their knees before 9 a.m. and after 6 p.m. My mom is the most tremendous, loving, moral and fabulous person. Because she's there I can focus on my job."

—Rhonda Adams Medina

Wipe the drool off your chin. Yes, yes, I know, we don't all have fabulous moms willing to tackle full-time childcare for the second time in their lives. But I have heard a lot of attorneys say that they have chosen to live near their parents and families so that they can take advantage of some assistance with childcare. So if that's an option for you, it's a good one to consider.

The point is that work/life balance isn't a simple equation, nor does the same approach work for everyone. You have to figure out what work/life balance means to you and then create a system for it. Try it out, make adjustments, revise it, make adjustments. . . .

CHAPTER 11

Counting the Hours, Minutes, and Seconds

"If your success is not on your own terms, if it looks good to the world but does not feel good in your heart, it is not success at all."

—Anna Quindlen

You joined the firm. You've been there six months, a year, two years, five years (you fill in the blank), and the glow of this accomplishment has definitely worn off. And you're starting to think, do I really want to do this? Do I want to stick it out for ten years or more to achieve partnership?

That can be an icky feeling. You've worked so hard to get here. Everyone is so proud of you. If you can just stick it out, you can have prestige, intellectual stimulation, a fat salary, and all the glory that comes with partnership.

But you've got this sneaking suspicion that you don't want to stick it out. What in the world are you going to do?

The first thing to do is not panic. Yes, yes, I know that's the easiest thing to do but it's the least helpful. Consider trying on a new perspective. Yes, panicking about the situation you've gotten yourself into is one perspective. Another is that you're about to embark on yet another exciting set of twists and turns in your career.

Carve out some time from your busy schedule, find a tall, shady tree to sit under, and let's look at some strategies for approaching this challenge.

Note: Here is where my expertise as a lawyer-turned-career-coach-for-lawyers really comes in handy. A lot of the strategies you'll see in this chapter come from my clients' experiences of making career transitions, not to mention my own.

Strategy #1: Diagnose what's wrong— is it the work, the practice group, the firm?

At this early stage, I like to keep it simple. With clients, I ask them to pull out a legal pad, draw a line down the center of the page, and write "Likes" on the left and "Dislikes" on the right. Then think about what you like and dislike about practice, your firm, and your group and write it down.

Once you've done that, take a look at the list. If you can do this step with a supportive friend, it's even better. What do you see?

Perhaps all of your likes tend to be grouped around a certain category and your dislikes, the same. For example, perhaps you like the nature of your work but you realize it's the people in your group that are driving you nuts.

There are a couple of different solutions for that. If your group is large enough, you can seek out folks you like and start asking them for work on a regular basis. In other words, you can make a gradual shift from doing work with people you don't like to people you do like. Just that small shift can make a drastic difference in your perception of the situation.

Here's another example: Maybe you don't like the nature of your work. You thought you wanted to be a litigator because it looked so glamorous on TV. Remember the TV show *L.A. Law*? That TV show may be too far back for some of you. How about *Ally McBeal*?

Don't laugh. A lot of people make career decisions based on bizarre information. According to the *New York Times*, applications for law school rose dramatically in 1988. The *New York Times* stated, "Explanations for the increase in applications range from the Oct. 19 stock market collapse, which may have tarnished the allure of a career on Wall Street, to 'L.A. Law,' the popular television program that glamorizes the lives and work of upscale lawyers." While others in the article disagreed with this analysis, June Thompson, the then-Associate Admissions Director at Harvard Law School, was quoted as saying, "'*There have been a number of events that have increased attention about what lawyers do,' said June Thompson . . . in trying to explain why the school has received almost 1,000 more applications this year, about 7,000, than it did last year for 540 openings. 'And who knows? Maybe it is L.A. Law.' "*[1]

So you realize you don't want to be a litigator. Or maybe you got put into a practice group that wasn't your first choice. And now you realize it's, like, the worst possible choice.

You really like your firm though. So start doing a bit of undercover research on some of the other practice groups. If you know folks in those groups, that's a great place to start. Swear them to secrecy and ask them some informational-interview type questions:

- What do you like about what you do?
- What do you dislike about what you do?
- What's a typical day good day like?
- What's a typical bad day like?
- What do you see for the future of this field?
- How would you recommend someone get into this field?

When I worked at a Big Firm, I watched one of my classmates do just this. He gathered information about a different practice area, evaluated his own interests and strengths to see if they were compatible with that type of practice, approached the head of the new practice group with a friend in the group, and essentially interviewed. A few months later, he made the shift and was much happier as a result.

One more example: You realize that it's Big Firm life that's bringing you down. A good friend recently left her large firm for a small one and is going on and on about how great her boutique is. Check it out, ask her lots of questions to see if the fit would be a good one for you (just because she says it's a great place doesn't mean it would be a great place for you), and see what you think. You've got a great "in" since you have a friend there. If they're hiring, get your friend to talk you up and go interview. That's actually how I made my transition from Big Firm to small firm.

Strategy #2: Figure out if you need to change your environment or if you need to change . . . you

"Women want to go in and fix everything. Sometimes it can't be fixed. You have to work within the system.

---

[1] http://www.nytimes.com/1988/04/01/us/the-law-law-school-applications-up-sharply.html

107

It's picking your battles, where you want to put your energy. Diverse associates get so frustrated, [what they're frustrated about] becomes a truth. Try to get perspective. If you've got good mentors, ask them, 'Why am I not getting x, y, and z? Is there something I need to learn?' Try to work through some of these issues.

Men are not going to worry about it. Women fret about it. It's not helping. Get perspective.

—Lisa Kobialka

Are you getting caught up in everything? Maybe you need to take a step back and figure out what the important battles are and then let the rest of it go. It's enough just doing the work, building relationships inside the firm and with clients, and handling the politics. Is it worth what little energy you have left to fret over things that you can't control?

And notice Kobialka's point that you can worry about something so much that you turn it into a truth. Things aren't always black and white. Maybe it's just a question of perspective. And that's hard to get on your own sometimes; so that's why it makes sense to pull in a mentor to help you think some of these issues through.

Remember the partner's comments in Strategy #4, Chapter 10: Develop a thicker skin. Take a walk around the block to vent with a friend, go cry in the bathroom, call someone who will remind you of how great you are. Do whatever you need to do to get it out of your system and move on.

Strategy #3: Deal with the difficult person who's making your life a living hell on earth

Maybe you've got a challenging person who is ruining your life. My heart goes out to you. I have faced this particular challenge a few times in my career.

Dealing with a difficult person is a book topic in and of itself. There have been lots of books written about that subject matter. Go out and find them and read them.

I'd also consider sharing your concerns with someone trustworthy, whether it be a more senior associate in the group, one of your mentors, or the Diversity chair. What you need is some guidance as to how to handle this person.

If there's someone in your practice group you feel comfortable with, I'd start with them. They may have the same opinion that you do, which is comforting in and of itself, but what they also may have, that you don't have, is a few years under their belt of dealing with this person. They can offer you some specific strategies for how to cope.

I've grown more assertive, as I've gotten older. And by assertive I don't mean aggressive. There is definitely a difference:

> "The Oxford English Dictionary tells us that the word assertiveness derives from the verb 'to assert,' which, according to those Oxford folks, means 'to state an opinion, claim a right, or establish authority.' They go on to say that if you assert yourself, you 'behave in a way that expresses your confidence, importance, or power, and earns you respect from others.'
>
> Let's differentiate that from aggressiveness, which means 'characterized by aggression: inclined to behave in an actively hostile fashion.' "[2]

Being aggressive is a strategy that only works for the super-audacious and those who are willing to take big risks.

What I've learned how to do is to assert myself so as to protect myself from the vagaries of difficult people.

First, it helps to figure out what's driving the behavior. After years of dealing with difficult people (and yes, I've had the pleasure of dealing with them in all of my jobs), I've discovered that first I have to understand what's going on for them.

Let's go back in time to when I used to practice and talk about Diana, a senior associate in my practice group, as an example.

Note: As much pleasure as I might derive from "outing" some of the not-so-nice people I've worked with in the past, I know better than that . . . and you should too. Never badmouth anyone in public. (Behind closed doors with trusted friends is a different story.) Thus, Diana is not a real person. She is a composite of some of the difficult people I've worked with.

Diana is micromanager. She is constantly peering over my shoulder and critiquing what I do. She also likes to call me into her office for worthless meetings. And when she reviews my work, it invariably comes back covered in red ink.

Diana is not sure whether the partners in her group like her and deem her worthy of partnership. She deals with her own precarious state by taking it out on younger associates.

---

[2] http://www.management-issues.com/display_page.asp?section=opinion&id=2697

Now Diana's not all bad. When she's in a good mood, she's very pleasant to be around, so much so that when her mood shifts, it can catch you off guard. In fact, you have to be careful not to let that friendliness lead you to divulging confidences about yourself. She will stab you in the back with those confidences if given the opportunity.

She'd be <u>astonished</u> though to hear that you don't like her. She thinks that she's an excellent manager and even a good friend. She has no clue how others perceive her and thinks that's she's the life of the party.

Diagnosis: Diana is insecure and lacks self-awareness.

Surprised? Don't be. There are lots of senior people walking around your firm who are a barrel of insecurities. That they lack self-awareness is probably less of a surprise. How one profession attracts so many people with a lack of social skills is beyond me. But I digress.

OK, you've done your diagnosis. Now what?

You've got to think strategically here. She's not leaving and you can't drop-kick her off of a cliff. You've got to figure out some way of working with her.

First, enlist the support of others in the same boat. If Diana rubs you the wrong way, I guarantee you she's having that effect on others. Do a little quiet digging and figure out who else is suffering. Or it may be obvious since they're in your office complaining about her right now.

As a group, you have to agree that you are going to take charge of this situation. You are going to "train" Diana to work better with all of you. You have to make a pact about this because if any one person caves, the strategy falls apart.

In my case, my friends (or as I liked to call them, "co-conspirators") and I decided that we would train Diana using a simple 2-step strategy: (1) reward "Good Behavior" and (2) refuse to tolerate "Bad Behavior."

Let me give you a few examples.

Diana assigns you and a co-conspirator to manage a project. You do the research, write the initial memo, and pass it off to your co-conspirator, who's a bit more senior than you to review it. Your co-conspirator reviews it carefully, makes a few changes, and then passes it on to Diana. Diana reads it and makes a few changes of her own. You review the changes, give them to your secretary to make, and the final document goes to the client.

I told you Diana has her good moments. Here she has avoided her tendency to over-manage and has let you and your co-conspirator do your jobs. How do you reward this good behavior? During the project and after the project, you and your co-conspirator let Good Diana know how much you enjoy working with her, how nice it is to work with someone who doesn't micro-manage projects and trusts the associates to do a good job. You thank her for involving you on such an enjoyable project.

Believe me, Good Diana hears what you're saying. She may not think that you're talking about her alter ego when you mention the micro-manager but she recognizes that such people exist. And she doesn't want to be one, especially if it means the people under her enjoy working with her and look forward to the next project. She's taking notes, I assure you.

But then Diana has a horror movie moment where her head does a 360° spin and she becomes Evil Diana. You're headed out of town early on a Friday and have cleared it with the partners you work with. You're working on a project with Diana and you sense that the fact that you're leaving the office early for a fun weekend bugs her. How do you know? Because she's hovering, questioning your every move on the project, marking up drafts, you suspect, just to create busy work. You make what you consider to be the final changes (because you are *not* missing your plane) and give her the draft, letting her know that it's the final. You hop a taxi and make it to the airport just in time to make your flight.

But where's the evil, you ask? Oh just wait. While you're gone, Diana is making mischief. She's in the hall with your co-conspirator(s). A partner from your group walks by. She says (loudly), "I hope Monica made her flight OK. She was in such a hurry to get out and I understand that but I think it's important that we do a good job for the client. So I'm not going to rush to get something out, especially if it's not perfect."

How is it I know that Evil Diana said this? Because, remember, I have a pact with my co-conspirators and they are sure to let me know when I return.

Now what do you do? Because this is "Bad Behavior." And you can't tolerate Bad Behavior because otherwise you're reinforcing it.

This is where you have to be willing to be bold. Let me preface this part of the story by saying that I had the reassurance that I was well-liked by the partners, as well as my fellow associates. And I knew that my co-conspirators had my back.

So after hearing about the lunchtime incident, I sent Diana an email. The reason I make first contact by email is because I want to craft what I'm saying carefully, I want to be able to say it without being interrupted, and I want it in writing. If this thing blows up into something larger, I want my side of the story in print. (Each situation may call for a different approach. You have to evaluate the situation to determine what is prudent.)

I simply write, "Diana, I heard that you said (the following) and the partner in charge most likely couldn't help but overhear you. My work product and my reputation are extremely important to me. I made sure to complete an excellent work product before leaving the office. So the insinuation that I was rushing to get out and did not do my best work is unfounded. I would appreciate it if in the future you refrained from making those kinds of comments. I look forward to talking to you about this on Monday."

And I did look forward to it. You've got to psych yourself up the same way Sylvester Stone did in *Rocky* when faced with a tough match. Because the Diana's of the world are bullies; they can smell fear. They respect you more when you can stand up to them. (I first learned this at an early age by reading a book called *Mean Max*. It's about a kid who is constantly being bullied by, you guessed it, Mean Max, and has to learn how to stand up to Max. I highly recommend it for you and your kids.)

What did Diana do on Monday when I went to talk to her about the situation? She denied it. She denied she'd said it. She asked me who told me. Again, because my co-conspirators and I had agreed on our strategy, they were willing to take a stand with me. So I told her who told me. She denied it again.

"Well, how's that a triumph?" you ask. "She didn't admit what she did and she didn't apologize." I don't need her to admit it or apologize. Remember, that's not my goal. My goal is for her to understand that I'm not going to tolerate that kind of behavior and consider that there are unpleasant consequences when she behaves that way.

When you are dealing with a difficult situation, you have to keep your eyes focused on the goal. The goal isn't always for someone to admit wrongdoing or to apologize or to feel bad. It's to get the person to stop exhibiting Bad Behavior. Admissions of guilt and apologies are irrelevant.

Now does that mean Diana was as sweet as cotton candy to me thereafter? No. But then, my job isn't to change Diana; that's an impossible task. My job is to protect myself.

Warning: This is a risky strategy. You have to think about what the consequences might be. In my case, I knew I was well-liked by the powers-that-be, that they were aware of Diana's shortcomings, and that I had the support of my co-conspirators. I was very careful to make sure that my own behavior was above reproach so that if I did have to explain or defend myself, I would be able to do so. I also made sure to document each incident so that I had a record.

Not everyone should take advantage of this strategy.

Strategy #4: Grin and bear it

The cadets at the Citadel have a saying: "Suck it up." It means exactly what it sounds like—if something is getting you down or you're finding it too hard, tough. Learn to deal with it.

It works in an environment like the Citadel. It's hot, close quarters; a regimented schedule; no means of escape (unless you want to quit). Sucking it up is a useful strategy under the circumstances.

We have a similar strategy in the law. It's called "Grin and Bear It." That means that no matter what someone does to you or what gets dumped on you, you just grin and bear it. My guess is that the theory behind this strategy is that nothing lasts forever. You will get past whatever obstacles are thrown in your path if you can just grit your teeth and persist.

You're probably wondering why I put this strategy last, thereby labeling it the riskiest. What's so risky about grinning and bearing it? Well, I believe that taking in a load of crap and internalizing it eventually has consequences. As we say in the conflict resolution training work I do, when Bambi meets Rambo, Bambi is sweet and innocent and Rambo is, well, Rambo. If Bambi and Rambo continue to meet up and Bambi continues to get slaughtered, Bambi is going to wise up at some point. That means Bambi is going to become Rambo eventually.

Unless Bambi comes up with some coping techniques. Grinning and bearing it is not a coping technique.

Either you end up taking on some of the unappealing characteristics of your nemesis or you internalize that bad stuff. Internalizing conflict results in headaches, migraines, stomach upset, ulcers, heart attacks. I think you understand my meaning.

You've got to find some way to get it out of your system. Whether it's venting to a friend, taking a kickboxing class, or meditating, you need a regular and consistent approach for flushing the toxins out of your system.

As one partner said:

> *"I'm an overly sensitive person. I personalize everything. To survive, I had to realize that some people are just nasty. I had to learn not to internalize it because I wouldn't make it. It [the Big Firm] can be a completely harsh environment if you allow it to be."*

> —Anonymous Attorney

Her coping mechanism is her family:

> *"I have a really close-knit family so I find a lot of strength in that. My father is very calm and consistent. When I feel bad, I call him. He's a sooth-*

113

ing person. My mom is there. So when I feel isolated, I call them. My family, my husband and my parents."

—Anonymous Attorney

You're not the only one with doubts about this path you've chosen

It can be hard sometimes looking at these superstar partners I've been interviewing, I know. You're thinking, "Man, they always know exactly what they want and how to go about getting it." You wonder if they have ever had doubts about going on this path to partnership. Of course they did!

Here's what one partner had to say:

"Hell yeah I had doubts. Daily. I still do. This was a 2—4 year plan. I was never supposed to be here this long. It was a fluke.

I can't wait to get out of the law firm. It's not my future. But whatever game I'm playing, I play to win. No one knows. They think I'm trying to have a five million dollar practice and rule the world. Perception is everything."

—Anonymous Attorney

Surprisingly, this partner wasn't the only one who told me that she hadn't planned on making partner from the start. I say "surprisingly" because I assumed that most, if not all, of these women came to the firm with stars in their eyes.

"When I started, I wasn't sure that I wanted to stay here and make partner. In fact, I probably thought that I wasn't but I always felt that the opportunity was there if I wanted to. So when I started it, I really liked it, I really liked the work I was doing, I liked the people. I just did the work and was happy here for the first several years.

And then . . . I had a period where I was working really, really hard and it was really, really crazy and it was stressful for two, three years. So at that period I started to think about, do I want to do this. And I had a couple of other opportunities to leave.

But at that point I decided not to because I was so close to making partner and I had done everything I was supposed to have done to make partner. It didn't seem prudent to walk away at that point—financial considerations and just time invested. So I said to myself, 'Let's put your nose down. Let's get this done. Let's make partner and then you can decide what you want to do after that point.' So then I did that.

And then I had a child the year after I made partner. . . . That period until not so long ago [2–3 years] was really hard. Because the traveling, the depositions, the hearings—and those are stressful things that require a ton of work and preparation. You've got this little baby that you want to spend time with, who needs you. That was very, very hard.

And so naturally during that period I was like, 'Hmm . . . Do I want to do something else? I did make partner, I stayed here, I've helped people along, I've done some things I wanted to do, I've helped the diversity initiative. Maybe it's time for me to go elsewhere.'

And frankly God apparently wants me to be right here for now. And so I recently made peace with that."

—Anonymous Attorney

And another one:

"I never really intended, I didn't have a career path of becoming partner. In fact, when I went to the firm I was thinking I would stay two years and get the big law firm experience and then do something else. I guess I always thought I'd do something with the United Nations. I went to law school thinking I'd be a human rights advocate for women and children.

I guess once I started at the firm, I just got sidetracked for so long. [laughs] And in terms of getting on this path, by the time you stay five years you think, well, gee, I've invested this much time for what, then I guess you start trying to make partner. It kind of just stumbled upon me in that way. I never left law school saying, 'Oh I'm going to make partner.' Over time that's just kind of how things developed.

And in terms of doubt, I think this is my whole work/life balance [issue]. I think that's one of my biggest struggles. [This partner has small children.] If I have any doubt, it's that. Am I doing the right thing? But I guess if my daughter sees me working, that's also self esteem for her. So I try to comfort myself that way."

—Anonymous Attorney

Here's another:

"Well, yes, [I have doubts] but for family reasons. I strongly encourage you, if you're thinking about making partner, to interview somewhere else. I interviewed elsewhere my sixth year. I couldn't imagine leaving here for that. That's good to know.

Everyone has to have doubt. It's a huge commitment."

—Anonymous Attorney

115

And another one:

> *"Of course I do. It's really, really hard. Playing in a man's sandbox. Very political. A lot of those things get to me that don't get to my [male] peers.*
>
> *Unfortunately there are so few minority women partners. They're generally so dispersed. I don't get this kind of contact. I know the issues are the same. I've never worked in an office where there is another woman [of color] partner.*
>
> *I've seen so many minority women say, 'Forget it. It's not worth it.' They go in-house, stay at home, do different things. Very few come back."*

—Anonymous Attorney

Is there a life outside of the Big Firm?

Maybe your dissatisfaction is larger than what I described above and you've come to the conclusion that it's firm life altogether that's bringing you down. Believe it or not, there is a whole world of opportunities outside of the firm. Government, public interest, in-house counsel. Here are a few strategies to get you going.

Strategy #5: Consider your timing

While there are no hard-and-fast rules as to when it is a good time to leave the Big Firm (after all, it depends on what your next step is going to be), here are some helpful guidelines from an executive legal search expert:

> *"Typically, attorneys become most marketable for lateral opportunities between their third and fifth years of practice, for both firm and in-house opportunities. However, after the sixth year of practice, lateral-ing to another firm tends to be a tad more challenging, as the firms have already started shaping and mentoring the partnership candidates from that class.*
>
> *Conversely, the amount of in-house opportunities increase as an attorney becomes more senior. For instance, there are ordinarily far more in-house opportunities for an attorney with 6-10 years of experience than there are for an attorney in her third year of practice.*
>
> *I always advise junior attorneys to practice at a firm for at least four or five years, if possible. This ensures that the attorney's legal training has provided her with a solid command of her practice area, and prepared her to ably advise a corporation and/or manage outside counsel."*

—Carolyn Pitt-Jones, J.D., Principal,
Ansun Management Partners, Atlanta, GA

116

Strategy #6: The dreaded "N" word: Networking

There are certain words that strike terror into the heart of even the most courageous woman. If you're not a social butterfly, networking just doesn't appear on your list of favorite activities. In fact, it may be akin to getting a root canal.

Here's why it's so important though:

"You need to network because postings of jobs don't always go out. They're on an internal email list posted in-house. It's because they're looking for someone with in-house experience. But that doesn't mean only those with in-house experience are hired. So buddy up."

—Bettina Yip

Not convinced?

"Networking is extremely important. When you see a posting and apply online, that HR person who doesn't know you needs at least a friend of a friend [to put in a good word for you]. It's better if someone can vouch for you, can say, 'She has a good reputation.' Reputation counts for so much."

—Bettina Yip

Still not interested in attending functions and handing out your business card? There are other ways to network. Yip is a master at them.

"I've been in leadership positions in bar associations. My name is all over the Internet. Recruiters see that. My name is on the Georgia Asian Pacific American Bar Association website year after year.

I'm willing to get out there and meet people. I get invited to speak on panels and at conferences. Some people think I'm a self-promoter but I don't think I am. I like to meet people and I like to talk."

—Bettina Yip

You've got to network.

Look at it this way: As much as you might like to be totally self-sufficient, it's just not possible under these circumstances. You cannot find and get a job completely on your own. Someone has to tell you about the job (or if it's a job posting online, someone's got to put in a good word for you); then there's the person to whom you send your resume; and there's the person (or persons) who interview you. You've got to rely on people sometime. You might as well start doing so at the beginning of the process so that you improve your chances of getting the position.

You can network your own way. You don't have to do the traditional stuff, like going to receptions and networking meetings. Get to know people in a way that feels comfortable for you. Join a legal association. Volunteer for a committee. As social as I am, I get shy in large groups of people. That's why I like to volunteer to host or run events. If I'm in charge, I feel as if it's my duty to welcome other people and make them feel comfortable. My role helps me to shift my perspective to a more positive and purposeful one.

Another way to shift perspective is to focus on giving instead of getting. If you see getting to know people as a way of getting them to do something for you, I can see why that might feel disingenuous. Instead, just think of a time when you're out having fun and you meet someone you like. You've got no agenda. Like Yip, perhaps you just like people and you like to talk. Build relationships that way. Be of service to them if you can. Help connect them with someone they need. That's what building relationships is all about. And then when the time comes that you need their help, the relationship is already there, and they're happy to help.

> *"The common thread . . . is relationship building. Having a large and diverse network has enabled me to hear about attorney positions very quickly, often when they are not yet publicly posted. Every attorney should find ways to network within the legal community, both within and outside of affinity Bar organizations."*

> —Carolyn Pitt-Jones

Strategy #7: Make the most of your current job

Yes, yes, I know, you've got one foot out the door already. But hang on a second. Stop and ask yourself the question, "What do I need to learn before I leave? What can I get out of this opportunity?" Hard questions to answer if you're ready to go, but they're very important. Remember, you do have a tremendous advantage being at the Big Firm. Don't squander that.

> *"Take full advantage of the bounty of resources that that unparalleled training ground provides. This includes mentors (assigned or informal), knowledgeable support staff, the law library, and many other resources that smaller firms, corporations, and government jobs are less likely to maintain. And learn as much as you can about your practice area—and other practice areas if possible.*

Finally, develop relationships with other attorneys at all levels, and make sure that you remain in touch. Many of them will move on to opportunities in firms and corporations that may interest you in the future."

—Carolyn Pitt-Jones

Strategy #6: Get clear about what you want from your work

"Figure out what you want. Don't just do what people think you're supposed to do. Find out what each position means, what you want to do. First figure out what's important to you and do those firms, companies fit."

—Bettina Yip

If you don't know what you want, how are you going to get it? That lack of clarity is yet another aspect of the job search that baffles me: people just looking to see what's out there without considering what they want. And then being surprised when they're not happy with what they get.

When I changed firms, I made a list of exactly what I wanted: a lower billable hours requirement, no mandatory "face time," colleagues who could become friends, a culture that valued family and an outside life, the same (or a better) salary. I remember a friend laughing at me saying, "What are you getting your hopes up for? You can't guarantee you're going to get all of that." Well, actually I did get all of it. That doesn't mean that you'll get what you want every time, but how can you get any of it if you don't know what it is?!

Lawyer by Default

What if your dissatisfaction runs even deeper? What if—dare I say it—you're thinking that you don't want to practice law anymore?

Some of you are lawyers by default, you know. You went to law school because you didn't know what else to do. All you knew was that you wanted a second degree, you wanted some prestige, and you wanted to make some money. Law seemed like a sure route for that.

You may have had doubts about practicing as early as 2L year. You got your first summer clerkship under your belt and thought, "Man, I don't know if I'm cut out for this." But you felt like such an oddity, you kept quiet. After all, everybody was else was practically gleeful about the six-figure corporate law opportunities being waved under their noses. Who were you to disagree? You figured you'd go check it out for a few years, pay down your loans, and then make a decision.

119

Maybe you make it through those first few years or maybe you don't. I've worked with a number of lawyers who had doubts about whether they want to be a practicing lawyer. In fact, I was one of them.

When I graduated from law school, I joined a terrific firm. I was in a sexy practice area and I was getting good work. But I wasn't happy. And I knew it wasn't the firm. I was coming to grips with the fact that I didn't enjoy the actual practice of law.

As I was wrestling with what to do, I was offered a lectureship at my alma mater, Harvard Law, to teach negotiation for a semester. (While I was a student in law school, I had seriously considered working in the conflict resolution field, instead of practicing law. I had been a teaching assistant for the negotiation course and had worked on a few projects with some of the teaching team.) I knew that if I accepted the lectureship, the year after I completed my semester of teaching would be my window of opportunity to pursue additional conflict resolution work in the corporate arena. I decided to leave the practice of law and pursue that career path. I had fun teaching for a semester, and then did corporate training work with some of the conflict resolution consulting companies affiliated with the law school.

But ultimately I went back to the practice of law. I was afraid that I hadn't given it a fair shot and that if I stayed out for too long, it would be hard to get back in and I would regret my choice.

Note: If you're like me, you might read that statement above and assume that it's the gospel truth, that if you leave the law too early, you haven't given it a fair shot—just because I wrote it. Just because I feared those things doesn't mean that they're real and absolute. Before assuming that what I said above is true in your case, do your research. Talk to people you trust, including perhaps a couple of legal recruiters, and then use your best judgment.

I joined a boutique firm and even changed practice areas (from IP Litigation to Employee Benefits). I practiced for four more years before I was ready to acknowledge that I didn't want to be a practicing lawyer.

Perhaps you're having similar doubts or you've even reached the definite conclusion that you don't want to practice. What's a girl to do then?

Let's look at how a few associates made their transition from Big Firm life to careers in, outside, and around the law.

Anita Raman leaves the law firm for the U.S. Attorney's Office

Anita Raman started her legal career at Cravath, Swaine & Moore LLP in litigation. After 2 1/2 years she switched to what was then a boutique,

Quinn Emanuel Urquhart Oliver & Hedges, LLP. After two years there, Raman joined the U.S. Attorney's Office in New Jersey.

Note: Raman is no longer at the U.S. Attorneys' Office; she is now a full-time mommy with two small boys. Needless to say, our focus will be on her transition from private practice to government practice. Transitioning from practice to full-time parenthood is a whole other book.

Q: How do you make the most out of your firm jobs before leaving?

"It's something I thought a lot about at the boutique firm. At the time there were ten lawyers total, five more senior. Three of five had just come from the Southern District. They loved the U.S. Attorney's Office. They were very gung ho about it.

A lot of people from Cravath made that move too.

No government job teaches you anything. They assume that you know how to be a lawyer. I learned from Cravath to take pride in my work, a very important lesson.

Be aware of your skills. Some firms are good at [associate development]; some are not. Making sure that associates have done all the things they should be doing—taking depositions, writing enough, making arguments.

Don't assume the firm will do it. Take it upon yourself. Writing, oral (doesn't even have to be advocacy because how often do you get to do that at big firms, even talking to opposing counsel, the court), being able to represent the client. Be conscious of those things. When you're not getting enough, speak up. In my experience, firms are perfectly happy to accommodate you when you're asking for work.

If you never ask, I feel like you can't complain if you don't get."

Q: How did you look for opportunities?

"If you're looking for any government positions, the government has a great website: usajobs.gov. The only thing is I don't think the U.S. Attorneys post there. Your best bet is to call the Offices. Often they're looking for one person; it's not like a firm—[firms] hire at a set time, they're able to fit people in. The Offices have websites; they do post [jobs] on there.

If you know people at the Offices . . . that helped me. They have a notoriously slow application process, even if they say they're hiring. It can take up to six months. I had a very good friend at the New Jersey Office. She just told me the person in charge of hiring. She told me to call him. She gave me his secretary's name. It helped to speed it along. He's got 800 resumes on his desk. No harm in calling. The people working there are generally very nice, the support staff, everyone. The HR people are so nice. It's a real breath of fresh air compared to some jobs."

Q: When is it a good time to make a change?

"With respect to government work, the U.S. Attorney's Offices don't hire generally out of law school. They want you to have experience. I've known those who make the shift from three years up . . . Three years is a little on the low side.

Getting a job you don't like is the worst. No job you have is the only job. Why not look at a U.S. Attorney job?

Look to switch when you're ready, figure it out from there. If you're done [practicing] after a year, figure out who will hire you. I knew this tiny woman (I'll explain why I said 'tiny') at Cravath. She started an internet company for petite women for clothes.

Q: What's so good about making the shift from private practice to government practice?

"The most obvious is that you don't have to bill time. [laughs]

It's much more supportive, collegial. It really is a team. There's a wealth of experience, people are happy to share it. Anyone would listen to you giving a cross examination, a direct examination, examining witnesses. It's an amazing thing.

The firms I was at were perfectly nice. I have no beef with them. But with that said, the U.S. Attorney's Office is a whole different kettle of fish. What they do at the U.S. Attorney's Office is really important. Firms think what they do is so important, the deadlines are so important, everything is a fire drill. The U.S. Attorney's Office is not like that at all but it's very important work.

You end up being slightly better off because you're working fewer hours. Now when you're on a trial, you have to be there. Even on trial, you're not there past 9:00. That's a pretty light day at a firm. [laughs] It's much better.

What's expected of you is to do your work and be your own boss. Your job is to move cases along. You're the only one to file, the only one to schedule. In that area it's a much bigger responsibility. There's a lot of autonomy. Coming from a firm that's a great change.

Everything you're doing is necessary. At firms there's some amount of [work], you don't always get the big picture for why you're doing something. Or you're given a piece of one part of a brief to write. You don't always get the feeling that what you're doing is necessary. At the U.S. Attorney's Office you're writing the whole brief. . . . You know [what you're doing] is important and necessary, which you didn't always know [at the firm].

Rhonda Adams Medina leaves the law firm for business and legal affairs

Rhonda Adams Medina practiced for a year at a Big Firm in New York City doing securities and corporate work. Then she spent two years at a specialty boutique practicing entertainment law. Now she's the Senior

Vice President, Business and Legal Affairs, Deputy General Counsel, Nickelodeon/MTV Networks Kids and Family Group in New York, NY.

Q: How do you make the most out of your firm jobs before leaving?

"You need to not be thinking about the next step all the time. People sabotage themselves thinking about Plan B. You should focus on Plan A. Now that I'm a manager it's very clear to me when people are using something as a stepping stone. You should focus on and dedicate yourself to what you're currently doing. I worked very hard. I always worked as if the job at hand was the end game.

I was pretty focused on making sure that in addition to the work that the firm gave me, I got work I wanted to do. I may have done the Intellectual Property work for a client but by the same token I inquired and met with the partner doing pro bono work for the local ballet. I rallied to get the work for the record label.

That's really what I did to prepare myself to leave. I tried to kill it while I was there. Because they [employers] all know each other. The partners at the entertainment boutique knew the partners at the Big Firm. People at Nickelodeon know the partners at the entertainment boutique. They're completely interrelated.

Question: How did you look for opportunities?

"You have to let people know you're a candidate. It's difficult to do when you're working somewhere based on what [I told you above]. I went through the Princeton and Harvard alumni directories [Rhonda is an alumnus of Princeton University and Harvard Law School]. I highlighted everybody working in the area I wanted to work in. Email was not as prevalent yet so I cold called everybody. Now I'd use email. I asked for informational interviews. I wouldn't be too worried about them [your current employer] finding out. But you can be discreet.

I talked to people. I left a resume. It was all based upon who people knew. No alumnus was too old or too young, as long as they were doing what I wanted to do. You have to do your homework. People hate it when you show up and say, 'I want a job.' I was prepared. I'd ask, 'How do people find out about opportunities where you are?' 'What would make me weak candidate? If you look at my resume, what's the weak part of my resume?'

In a lot of companies all roads pass through HR. That's not necessarily a bad thing. Going through me, especially if it's not a Business Affairs position, can be like going through a black hole. You're better off giving your resume to HR with my thumbs up.

But who in HR? You don't want to give your resume to the most junior person. Different HR's have different levels of heft in companies and different HR people have different levels of power."

123

Question: When is it a good time to make a change?

"With in house, raises and promotions are not lock-step. Superstars can rise very quickly. For others, you start a certain level making a certain amount and you won't move much many years from now.

There are different opportunities at a young company. When I came to Nickelodeon, it was young in its life cycle. I had the privilege of being here when some of the structure within Business Affairs was still in transition. There's opportunity where there's transition. There are opportunities where there's not calcification.

I've been told that other Fortune 500 companies can be rather rigid. You come in making X amount of dollars with this title. You may get a very slight raise but the only time you'll get a different title is if somebody dies.

Based on that, there's a trend toward the argument that you should at least be at VP-level before you go in-house. You should have five years under your belt.

For me personally as a hiring person, I like two years of Big Firm experience. I hate seeing people who've jumped around too much. In Los Angeles, they like seeing that. If it's someone from the East Coast, I like to see that they're able to stay somewhere. It shows me that they're not always looking over your shoulder for the next opportunity."

Question: What's so good about making the shift from practice to in-house?

"The difference is profound. There is significantly greater job satisfaction with people who are in-house. I have the opportunity to be part of a team where we make a product, television. It is directly relatable to children and I'm a mom.

I don't function simply as a scrivener. I am really truly acting as counsel. I get brought in on things that have nothing to do with the law. I'm making a deal with an agent and business manager and the attorneys are brought in to paper the deal.

My view is more towards the deal-making process and the value I add is that I have a J.D. and can also paper it.

I see the big picture. I'm working with people from across various areas in the company. I work with the business-school trained Business Development group. I work with the people in Consumer Products. I work with the production people. I work with the people on the ground floor who say, 'That's great, Rhonda, but I have to get a show done.'

I think a lot of law is ivory tower. Thinking of ways deals can go wrong. . . . Here we have to get things done in real time. It's a much more interesting perspective.

I like helping a company that has a point of view and a perspective. I can get involved in so many different aspects. I can impact the product that's being made and have my voice be heard.

It's a significant lifestyle improvement for me."

J. Shontavia Jackson leaves the practice of law for legal academia

J. Shontavia Jackson spent two years as an Intellectual Property associate at a large firm in Greenville, SC. She is now a Professor of Law, Waterfield Fellow, at Loyola University College of Law in New Orleans, LA. Her specialty is the intersection of Intellectual Property and Human Rights.

Question: How do you make the most out of your firm job before leaving?

"Once I decided that [academia] was an option, I talked to law professors. I got recommendations from professors I had or knew or friends.

Within the firm, every attorney had a list of things they'd done in the past. Once I gave my letter of resignation, I talked to lawyers who taught a course, [etc.]. They had done some phenomenal things in the academic field. They gave me a lot of good advice.

One thing that was quite helpful—some of my former professors recommended I start writing articles in the field. One professor told me to start writing short blurbs to get my name out there.

I started reading, putting out feelers to people in the Human Rights community. There was a professor renowned for Human Rights work in the African Diaspora. He gave me topics to start thinking about, areas of expertise to make myself marketable.

Another good piece of advice—if I could make myself fit into a niche not a lot of others fill. There are lots of constitutional law scholars. In terms of Intellectual Property and Human Rights, most don't realize there is a connection, let alone an entire field of law."

Question: How did you find the program? It sounds like it was an independent study. [Jackson left her law firm without having a job offer. She had applied to a few schools to get an LLM and gotten accepted. She had also applied for a human rights program in South Africa.]

"Essentially that's exactly what it was. Now it's scary to look back. I was floundering.

I got on Google. I looked up human rights programs. I [saw one that looked like] a good choice. [It was the Comparative and International Law Program in South Africa offered by Howard University.] One [of the instructors] was a

125

*member of the South African Constitutional Court. That would be like study-
ing with a U.S. Supreme Court justice. Another was a former United Nations
attorney. She had done work during post-apartheid.*

I applied for the program."

Question: What it was like transitioning without a job? [Jackson was
accepted into the program. She thought that she would go to South
Africa and then come back and get an LLM.]

*"Scary. I went from making well over six figures to zero. Financially this
[leaving the law] was a terrible decision. But professionally it was probably the
best move I've made in the legal field.*

*When I left, I decided to go to South Africa but I had no plan post-Capetown.
I was there for four months. Right before I left, a week before I left, I got a call
from Loyola. [Before leaving for South Africa, Jackson had also attended the academic job fair in Washington, D.C. She had interviewed with schools and had
good callbacks. She had also interviewed with Loyola for a fellowship but had
not heard anything before she left.] This is crazy but the interviews I really liked
that were tenure track, once I thought about the way I wanted to market myself, I wasn't sure the schools would be that receptive. So I turned them down.
Like at the firm—I took [that job] thinking that I could make it work. But it was
less than conducive to my ultimate career goals. The [law school positions] paid
well, they were in a great part of the country, I just wasn't sure that they'd be
the right fit. I turned them down even though I was leaving the firm."*

Question: When is it a good time to leave the practice of law for aca-
demia?

*"Google has been my best friend. There are so many law review articles
about entering the academic field. The consensus from the professors [I talked
to] and articles is about three years. Generally after so much experience, say ten
or fifteen years, you're better suited maybe for a clinical professorship."*

Question: What's so good about making the shift from practice to ac-
ademia?

*"The last day of the semester is April 15. I don't have to go back to work
until August. I'm still working but I'm focusing on things I really want to do,
like scholarship and non-profit work.*

The schedule is a lot more flexible. I don't work 18–20 hours a day anymore.

*Once you get to the tenured track, the differences in salary [between prac-
ticing and teaching] won't be that great, if at all.*

*It's just better. I feel like I get to do more meaningful work, things I find more
meaningful."*

Nicole Pierre leaves the practice of law to become a lobbyist

Nicole Pierre practiced Labor & Employment law at two Big Firms, went in-house, all in Atlanta, GA and ultimately ended up transitioning out of the Legal Department at UPS into a Corporate Public Affairs Manager position (read as, lobbyist) at the company and moving to Washington D.C.

Question: How did you make the most of your legal job before you left?

"#1: I developed work competency.

I became proficient in Labor & Employment. I kept up with my CLE. I tried to get really good assignments with novel questions of the law. I did litigation-oriented assignments. I got good deposition skills and experience. I did a lot of class action work, a lot of depositions, motion-writing, arguing early on. It was unusual for a first year.

I was strategic about the partners I worked for. I looked for partners who were interested in developing associates, not just those who wanted a worker bee. The ones who take the time to critique your work, give you meaningful feedback. The ones who explain the process behind why you're making an argument. Those are the ones who could also make your life miserable because they're hard on you.

I also asked senior associates who's good to work for.

I had one or two mentors outside of the firm. I talked to them about skills-building and whether I was on track. I specifically chose Labor & Employment attorneys outside of the firm.

I also looked to senior associates. I was lucky in that the work team was great at both of my firms. People wanted you to succeed. I was looking to the older associates. That's also pretty critical.

#2: I developed relationships. I didn't realize I was doing this then. How to build relationships so that they trust me to take on additional experiences and forgive me for making mistakes.

It's showing up and hanging out. I went to everything. I went to summer associate events even when I was not a summer associate.

Going out for drinks. Going to parties at partners' houses. I played softball games even though I'm not athletic. I wanted to be seen as a team player. I got to know partners on a personal level.

I volunteered for committees [at the firm]. I gave feedback of things that could make the firms a better place.

#3: I always billed above the hours I was supposed to be billing.

Question: How did you look for opportunities outside of the firm?

[Pierre left her first firm for her second firm because the partners at the first firm were retiring and there was no succession plan. The partner that she did

most of her work for was headed to Alston & Bird. At that time, a headhunter called Pierre. She interviewed for a position at Troutman and received an offer.] I was going to Troutman. One night the partner [who was going to Alston & Bird] came into my office. I hadn't told anyone I was looking [for a job]. I said to the partner, 'I have to tell you I will probably not be far behind you.' For some reason I just said it. He said, 'Where do you think you're going?' I told him Troutman. He said, 'No, you're not.' That is how I got to Alston & Bird.

Really interesting because I was doing a lot of UPS work at the firm. That [the UPS work] was moving to Alston & Bird.

I made the transition to Delta Airlines because a headhunter called. I was not looking for a job. I didn't even have my resume ready.

I listened [to the headhunter] though because I was kind of tired of class actions. I knew what the next two years would bring to get on the partnership track. I was not really interested.

The headhunter said, 'Can we just talk? I like people who aren't looking.'

[Pierre interviewed and really liked the group she'd be working with.] I ended up leaving. It was really hard. I really liked Alston & Bird.

[For her second in-house job, which was with UPS, Pierre says that she was looking.] I was at Delta 2 1/2 to 3 months before 9/11. I loved the work. But morale was bad. I was worried about layoffs.

I called a headhunter. The headhunter set up a bunch of different interviews. I thought I was going to Bell South. Then on a final interview at Bell South, they told me they couldn't hire me because the Delta CEO sat on the Bell South Board.

That day Teri McClure [now Senior Vice President of Legal, Compliance & Public Affairs, General Counsel & Corporate Secretary] who was head of the Labor & Employment Group at UPS called me. She said she needed a lawyer. She had been my mentor for two years. I said, 'What timing!'

Question: When is it a good time to make a move from a Big Firm?

It depends on what you want to do. I always made moves that didn't require a significant drop in pay.

I always thought five years was a good time. If you tried to move as a partner, unless it's an assistant General Counsel or General Counsel position, it's more difficult.

For lateral moves, as long as you've got a year or two under your belt. If it's really a bad fit, six months. It's less about the time and more about having a rationale for why you're leaving. And not doing it too many times because you look indecisive or as if you're a problem.

Question: What's so good about making the shift from practice to lobbying?

It's challenging in different ways. I use my legal skills as a lobbyist but I'm learning something new. It's fresh. It's like going back to school—learning political lobbying is like litigation without the Federal Rules. You're using powers of persuasion. You have to know the politics.

I'm never bored with what I do now. In Labor & Employment you tend to see the same types of cases."

Strategy #7: Learn the strategies for making a career change that no one ever taught you

Why figuring out what you want to do with your life isn't a course taught in high schools and colleges is beyond me. It's one of the biggest decisions you'll ever make and, yet, you're just supposed to pull an answer out of thin air. Bizarre.

Well, bizarre as it is, it means you have to play catch-up once you're an adult. It's time to learn how to make a career transition.

The 1-2-3 Career Counseling Process[3]

This approach comes courtesy of Richard Bolles, author of the perennial favorite, *What Color Is Your Parachute?* I like it because it gives you a simple approach to making a career transition.

Simple, by the way, doesn't mean easy. The formula is simple. And that's important because the more complicated it appears to you, the harder it is going to be for you to make a change. While the formula is simple, making a career change isn't necessarily easy. But I think it's crucial that you have a strategy that you can keep in your head and use as a road map so that you don't get lost in all of the minutiae. Here it is:

1. **What do I want to do?**
2. **What's stopping me?**
3. **What am I doing about it?**

Let's look at each step.

Step #1: What do I want to do?

Make a list of career possibilities that excite you. You don't have to be exact about it. Just get a sense of what appeals to you. It could be as general as cooking and as specific as pastry chef.

Skip the censor here. You know, that part of yourself that likes to tell you what you want is impractical, silly, not going to happen. The censor

---

[3] The Career Counselor's Handbook, Howard Figler and Richard Bolles (Ten Speed Press), p. 111

gets to take the stage in Step #2. So tell it to hold off and just make the list. Write 'em all down, both the practical and the impossible.

Go ahead. Do it now. I'll wait. I'll hum while you get it done. Hm hm ta dum tee dum. . . .

OK got it? Good.

Here's something interesting that you might see in your list. I saw it in mine. In her book, *Working Identity*, Herminia Ibarra points out that the list actually follows a pattern. The list contains some traditional ideas (for you, that would be practicing law somewhere else), some that are slightly different (possibly practicing in an arena that prizes legal skills), and then a few that are way out there (like owning a scuba diving shop in the Caribbean). The ones that really excite you, the ones that are way out there, are often buried near the bottom of the list. It's as if you can barely acknowledge them.

That's typically where I ask my clients to start the exploration process. With the stuff that excites them and makes them feel slightly nauseated. Why? Because it's probably what they really want to do and they just need a little encouragement. Go ahead. I give you permission to start your exploration there too.

Step #2: What's stopping me?

This is where the censor in you gets to go to town. There are all kinds of reasons, I am sure, why you can't pursue some of the careers on your list. I don't even need to prime that pump, I'll bet, because your censor is raring to go.

So let it loose. Go ahead and jot down all of the reasons you can't pursue some of the careers you listed. Get it out on paper.

Clients often ask me, "What's the point of this step? It's so demoralizing." Well, it's not the end of the process. We won't stop here. But we do need to get this stuff out of your head and onto the paper so you can move on. Once it's on paper, we can also assess it more clearly.

Get to work! Go ahead and write 'em down now.

Got your list? Excellent.

Step #3: What am I doing about it?

Now just as you said, if we stopped at Step #2, we'd be dead in the water. But we don't stop there because it's time for you to do a bit of analysis. It's time to reality check those obstacles.

Bolles describes two kinds of reality testing. The first kind is Reality Test Type A: Is the objection real? For example, your cousin Ruby told you it's going to cost you gobs of money to do interior decorating. That means you'll have to go back to school and take an exam. You've got enough debt already and no time to breathe, thank you very much.

But is that true? How accurate is your cousin's perception and how can you get better data? Do a little research. Start online. Here's what you'd find:

Well if you become an interior designer, yes, it's true you'd have to go back to school and take an exam. Maybe it's worth it to find out how much that would cost though and then make a decision. "Gobs of money" isn't exactly a precise determination.

There is an alternative though. If you decide to hang up your shingle as an interior decorator, no license is required. That means you could just take classes to build up your knowledge base and then just get started.

That's why you need to do Reality Test Type A. Don't just rely on what the naysayers around you are telling you. Go find out what the truth is. Heck, if there's one thing you learned in law school, it's how to research. Stop relying on the fuzzy, phony statistics that people who don't know what they're talking about give you and get some clarity.

The second kind of reality testing is Reality Test Type B. Let's say you find out that the obstacle is in fact a real one. The question then becomes, what can I begin to do to overcome that obstacle? If you're stuck on interior design (rather than decorating), you can investigate part-time programs. Maybe there's a school with courses you can take at night and on weekends. Perhaps there's a scholarship program. Or maybe you can find a grant.

Instead of just letting the weight of your obstacles crush you, figure out a way to get over, under, or around them.

Or . . . maybe not. You might feel after doing your research and thinking about ways to get around obstacles, or even starting to try to get around them, that the obstacles are too great. That's OK because you've got a list, remember? You weren't just looking at one possibility. You had other ideas that excite you. Go back to the list and go through the process again with another possibility.

By the way, going through the process is not necessarily a linear thing. You'll weave in and out of the three steps the entire time you're making your transition.

If you want more support than this, and I recommend you get it because the more you know, the less challenging making a transition becomes, here are a few more resources to get you started:

The Unhappy Lawyer: A Roadmap to Finding Meaningful Work Outside of the Law (Sourcebooks) by Monica Parker. That's right, that's me. I'm promoting my own work here. The book is a guide written especially for lawyers who want to explore alternative careers. It takes you from wherever you are, whether that be, "I don't have a clue what else I could do" or "I've got a list of possibilities but I need a bit more guidance," to exploring those possibilities without leaving your day job, to turning in your resignation letter. My favorite part of the book is that each chapter contains an in-depth interview with a lawyer who has transitioned out of the law.

Working Identity (Harvard Business School Press) by Herminia Ibarra. Ibarra does a wonderful job of proving her thesis that career change isn't about doing all of this internal work to come up with "It," the ideal career. Career change is actually a combination of internal work, exploring by taking on projects, and creating the storyline that allows you to believe that it's possible to leave the law and say, join a monastery. OK, Ibarra doesn't have a story about a lawyer doing that in her book, but there is another professional who makes that career change. Ibarra's premise is that making a career change is about more than moving from Point A to Point B. It's about changing your working identity and that's not always easy.

The Career Coward's Series (JIST Works) by Katy Piotrowski. This series walks you through each aspect of the career change process. You can start with *The Career Coward's Guide to Changing Careers* but other titles in the series are just as valuable because they cover topics like interviewing and resumes. I love the title "Career Coward" because that's certainly how I felt (and how a lot of my clients feel) about making a career change. Piotrowski acknowledges each of these fears and shows you strategies for dealing with them. My favorite sections of each chapter are "Panic Point!" which points out and troubleshoots areas that Career Cowards find particularly challenging, and "Career Champ Profile," which provides a real-life example of a Career Coward who succeeded after conquering a challenging career-change fear.

Strategy #8: Surround yourself with supportive people

Making a career change is not a one-man job. I don't recommend that you go it alone. Why? It's too hard. As we discussed above, we're talking about changing your working identity. You're going up against three years of law school and learning how to think like a lawyer, the bar exam, practice, and a lot of people's expectations ("You went to law

132

school and now you don't want to be a lawyer?!"). That's hard to handle by yourself. You're fragile enough about feeling this way; you don't need any additional boulders of doubt and fear crashing down around you. That'll just make you scuttle back into your dark, safe, albeit miserable, little hole.

That's why it's so important to find people who will support you on your journey. I recently told participants at a workshop that what you want are people who say things like, "You want to become a masseuse? Great!" not "Are you kidding?" You've got enough naysayers rotating around in your brain.

And if the naysayers are close to you, family or friends, that means you're going to have to learn how to keep your mouth shut around them. I can't tell you how many clients I've worked with who feel compelled to persuade their loved ones that they're doing the right thing. (I did this too when I was exploring making a career change.) If you're waiting for the people in your life to say, "You know what? You're absolutely right. Cut loose from that boring ol' law job and start up that adventure travel company!" you may be waiting a while. Love these people, respect them, cherish them, but find someone else to share your fragile, precious dreams with. Someone who can help you protect and grow those dreams, cheer you on, and give you a push when you need it.

And surrounding yourself with supportive people, well, that includes you! We can sometimes be our worst enemies. No more of this crap where you beat yourself with a stick because you've changed your mind about what you want to do with your life. So what? Here are your options: stay in the law and punish yourself *or* get out there, explore the possibilities, find something that engages you enough to make you want to get past the obstacles, and do it. Once you're on the other side, you won't care that you left the law. You'll be too happy!

Of course you can always work with a professional: a career coach, a career counselor, the alumni advisor at your law school, or join a career transition group (or create one of your own). I had supportive friends but I wanted more guidance. I wanted a partner who had nothing but my agenda on her mind and heart and would hold me to it. So I hired a coach and look what happened—I found so much value in the process that I became one!

You Are Not Alone

The main thing you should know is that you are not the first, nor will you be the last person dissatisfied with your legal career and/or the practice of law. Did you know that as 40,000 new lawyers enter the profession each year, 40,000 are on their way out?[4] It's practically a revolving door!

So take heart in the fact that you are not by yourself. There's no shame in leaving the practice of law. The shame is if you stick it out and spend the next several years of your life being miserable. I simply must refer you to this cliché: Life is short!

And if you're worried about what everyone will think if you leave, there are two distinct possibilities: (1) They'll think, "She's crazy!" or (2) They'll think "Man, I wish I was her!" If they think #1, who cares? Really, who cares? First of all, they are not you. They do not have to sit in your office every day suffering throughout the day because you're unhappy.

Second, once you *do* find work that makes you happy, they will be the first ones proclaiming at the top of their lungs that they knew you'd be much happier once you found your place. Trust me, I have personal experience with this one.

And of course if they're thinking #2, well, a lot of times they'll tell you. When I left the practice of law the first time, associates (and partners) I didn't even know came out of the woodwork to wish me well and tell me that they wished I could take them with me. That was a fun confidence booster.

---

[4] How Lawyers Lose Their Way: A Profession Fails Its Creative Minds, Jean Stefancic, Richard Delgado (Duke University Press, 2005)

CONCLUSION

"No one keeps up his enthusiasm automatically. Enthusiasm must be nourished with new actions, new aspirations, new efforts and new vision."

—Papyrus

My fervent hope for you at the end of this book is that you are feeling refreshed and renewed. That you are feeling inspired and hopeful.

One thing to remember from the stories shared here is that no one is perpetually enthusiastic about their work. You have to renew your commitment to your goals on a regular basis. It's that reflection and recommitment to what you want to accomplish that sustains you for the long term.

I've offered you a lot here. For some, it's a bit much to digest. Looking for a simple plan to follow? If you're anything like me, you're hoping it's here in this chapter. Here it is:

The 3-Step Plan

1. Figure out what you want and your deep "why's"
2. Create a plan to reach your goals but be sure to take into account the obstacles to achieving those goals
3. Follow the plan but be flexible

Let's take a look at each step.

Step #1: Figure out what you want and your deep "why's"

You aren't going anywhere (or at least not anywhere you want to go!) until you figure out what you want. What do you want for your work and life? Get crystal clear about it. Create your own mission statement. Not one of those namby-pamby ones that companies create. Make it a living, breathing, shiny thing that excites you so much that you can't wait to have it. And don't forget that you want more than just to accomplish your work goals. There are life goals as well: spirituality, health, family, friends, wealth, creativity, fun, balance, etc. Be sure to include those too.

And write it exactly the way you want. Shoot for the stars, my dear! This isn't the time to be "realistic." Don't worry—life and the naysayers in yours will take care of the realism. But for now, dream big.

Once you're clear on what you want, I think that you need to figure out *why* you want it. And it needs to be something deeper than prestige, money, and power. Those turn out to be pretty shallow "whys." They won't sustain you for the long term.

135

In his book *The Greatest Man Who Ever Lived*, Steven K. Scott talks about the importance of having deeper whys:

> *"Our levels of energy, creativity, productivity, perseverance, and passion will all be determined and empowered by our why. The greater the mission, and the more difficult and time-consuming it is, the deeper our why must be to help us achieve our goal successfully."*[1]

Personal gratification, money and material possessions, and the approval or "applause" of others won't be enough. Deeper whys include personal achievement, love, family, and connection to God.

Here is Allegra Lawrence-Hardy's deep why:

> *"For me it's all about the vision. I'm very clear why I'm here. I'm very well compensated, thank you, Lord. I developed a book of business to change the face of the legal profession. My being in a firm is my way of being the change. I believe I'm doing God's work.*
>
> *My mom is a computer science professor at Spelman College. I'd always say to her, 'Why don't you go work for IBM?' She'd say, 'My mission is to educate black women.' That really resonated with me. My mission is to help change the face of the profession.*
>
> *For me it really is—you have to do this work with a vision. You've got to have a mission."*

> —Allegra Lawrence-Hardy

You can see why Lawrence Hardy's deep whys have sustained her through all of the challenges of her career. Yes, the money is a blessing. But what she is saying, and countless others told me, is that money, prestige, and power won't be enough to sustain you on this immensely challenging journey. You have to have deeply personal whys that rest on personal achievement, love (whether it's as straightforward as love for your family or as grand as a love for humanity), and/or God (for those whose religious faith is at the core of their lives) to sustain you.

Once you're clear on what you want and your deep whys, write them down. **This is a very important step you do not want to skip.** For each of your wants, be sure to write them in the present tense, as if they have already happened.

---

[1] The Greatest Man Who Ever Lived: Secrets for Unparalleled Success and Unshakeable Happiness from the Life of Jesus, Steven K. Scott (Broadway Business, 2009), p. 52.

Take time often to speak out loud your wants and deep whys. **Another extremely important step.** Believe in your heart that it's possible. I like to read my big dreams out loud first thing in the morning and right before I go to bed so they are the first and last things my eyes, mind, and heart "see" and hear.

Note: If you are Christian, go to your Bible and find Scripture that supports your goals and speak that aloud too. Imagine how much more power you will have to achieve your goals with the Word backing you.

Step #2: Create a plan to reach your goals, but be sure to take into account the obstacles to achieving those goals

Once you've got your deep whys, you can think about the next step, which is creating a plan to achieve your goals. Without a plan, you're not doing much more than wishful thinking. Would you get on the road without having a map? How much more important is it then to have a map for your life plan? That's what this book has been all about. Strategies you can include in your plan.

This book has also been about the challenges. Thinking that you can make this journey without running into hardship is foolhardy and a recipe for disaster. Think about what your specific challenges might be and consider how to get around them.

Step #3: Follow the plan but be flexible

Once you've got the plan, follow it! Don't stick it in a drawer and forget about it. Keep it posted somewhere so you can see it.

The plan won't take into account everything. You will get new information as you go along and there will be challenges you won't anticipate. The plan is not written in stone; it's meant to be a living document. So absolutely you need to be flexible. Review it every so often and revise it as needed.

There. There's your 3-step plan. Yes, I said it was simple. Simple doesn't necessarily mean easy though, does it?

Final words of advice

I thought it would only be fitting to let the women I interviewed offer you some final words of advice.

> *"If you're trying to decide whether to go to law school, don't go to law school unless you want to be a lawyer. It costs too much, both in time and money.*

137

If you've decided you want to be a lawyer, try to get as much exposure as you can to practice areas so that you can pick one that fits with your personality.

Pick a firm that suits you."

—Sulee Clay

"Figure out what you want as early as you can. You don't want to wake up and be somewhere by default."

—Angela Payne James

"A lot of times associates feel powerless. You feel like you're in a little, dark corner. That's only if you see yourself as that. Everything you do is part of a joint effort and it's important. If you [treat it as if] it's important, it will lead to something. To master the small things doesn't diminish you at all."

—Rhonda Adams Medina

"The most important thing is to set goals. Figure out what you want and what you need to do to get there. Then go for it!"

—Danelle Smith

"Do or do not. There is no try."

—Yoda in the film *Star Wars.*

OK, OK, so Yoda wasn't a woman of color partner at a law firm. But didn't I tell you at the very beginning that we shouldn't be looking just for mentors that look like us?

EPILOGUE

Yes, we've come to the end of the book. But oh, is it just the beginning for you!

> *"Our deepest fear is not that we are inadequate. Our deepest fear is that we are powerful beyond measure. It is our light, not our darkness that most frightens us. We ask ourselves, Who am I to be brilliant, gorgeous, talented, fabulous? Actually, who are you not to be?"*

> —Marianne Williamson

ABOUT THE AUTHOR

Monica R. Parker helps lawyers create fulfilling careers and lives—in or outside of the law. Through her company, Parker provides the tools lawyers need to achieve career satisfaction, including individual coaching. She is a popular presenter at bar and legal associations, offering interactive, fun, and humorous keynote speeches that inspire her audiences. Parker is also the author of *The Unhappy Lawyer: A Roadmap to Finding Meaningful Work Outside of the Law* (Sourcebooks).

Before starting her company, Parker practiced law for five years, first at a Big Firm and then at a boutique. She also served as a Lecturer on Law at Harvard Law School teaching the Negotiation Workshop. She received her J.D. from Harvard Law School and her B.A. *cum laude* from Harvard College.

Prior to her legal career, Parker worked in grocery store management in Atlanta, GA and film development for Spike Lee at 40 Acres and A Mule Filmworks in Brooklyn, NY, and is still passionate about grocery stores and movies. She resides in Atlanta, GA.

Find out more at www.MonicaParker.com.

INDEX